THE KING JAMES
VERSION DEBATE

THE KING JAMES VERSION DEBATE

A Plea for Realism

D. A. CARSON

BAKER BOOK HOUSE
Grand Rapids, Michigan

Copyright 1979 by
Baker Book House Company

ISBN: 0-8010-2427-7

Library of Congress
Catalog Card Number: 79-50443

First printing, April 1979
Second printing, March 1980
Third printing, October 1981

PHOTOLITHOPRINTED BY CUSHING - MALLOY, INC.
ANN ARBOR, MICHIGAN, UNITED STATES OF AMERICA

Contents

Preface

This little book is not the sort of thing I like to write. Yet for a variety of reasons I have been called upon again and again to say something about English versions of the Bible; and it has therefore been impressed on me repeatedly that a short volume on the subject, written at an easy level, was sorely needed.

Dr. H. H. P. Dressler and Dr. J. B. Richards read an earlier draft and offered some helpful corrections, and I am grateful. Mr. Larry Perkins has been of the greatest assistance, and his advice most enriching. None of these men, however, should bear the brunt of whatever criticism the following pages evoke. My warm thanks, too, to Diane Smith and Pat Doidge, who reduced a messy manuscript to neat typescript.

Soli Deo gloria.

D. A. Carson
Vancouver, B.C.
Thanksgiving 1977

Abbreviations

BanT	*The Banner of Truth*
Bib	*Biblica*
BJRL	*Bulletin of the John Rylands Library*
BT	*The Bible Translator*
CT	*Christianity Today*
EQ	*The Evangelical Quarterly*
ET	*The Expository Times*
JBL	*Journal of Biblical Literature*
JETS	*Journal of the Evangelical Theological Society*
KJV	King James Version
LB	The Living Bible
LXX	Septuagint
MLB	Modern Language Bible
ms(s).	manuscript(s)
NASB	New American Standard Bible
NEB	New English Bible
NIV	New International Version
NJT	*Northwest Journal of Theology*
NTS	*New Testament Studies*
NWT	New World Translation (used by "Jehovah's Witnesses")
ODC	*The Oxford Dictionary of the Christian Church,* 2d ed.
RSV	Revised Standard Version
RV	Revised Version
TB	*Tyndale Bulletin*
TEV	Today's English Version
TNTC	Tyndale New Testament Commentaries
TR	Textus Receptus
WTJ	*Westminster Theological Journal*
ZNW	*Zeitschrift für die neutestamentliche Wissenschaft*

Introduction

Three historical realities make the topic I have chosen a hot one. The first is that the sixty-six books that make up the canonical Scriptures stand at the heart of Christian faith and practice. Christians everywhere recognize that discussion which touches these Scriptures touches a vital part of their faith; indeed, perhaps the most vital part. The second historical reality is the religious history of the church during the past two centuries. That history is bound up indissolubly with the way the Bible has been viewed. Evangelicals have therefore been sensitized to any deviation from an orthodox doctrine of Scripture; but some in their zeal have erected a fence around Christian Torah and seen deviations even where there are none. The third reality is the proliferation of modern English versions.

Evangelical reactions to modern English versions have varied from unqualified praise to equally unqualified condemnation. Both extremes are unjustifiable. Modern translations and modern paraphrases ought not be lumped together as if they were all of a piece.

There has arisen a sizable and vocal body of opinion that defends the King James Version (KJV) as the best English

9

version now extant. Some of these defenders merely argue strongly; but others have gone so far as to make the adoption of this view a criterion of orthodoxy. They dismiss those who dissent from them as modernists, compromisers, or dupes. I respect their desire to contend for the faith once delivered to the saints; but I disagree heartily with many of their conclusions and even more of their arguments.

Lest I be dismissed out of hand as another "modernist," I protest strenuously that when I sign the thoroughly conservative Articles of Faith of Northwest Baptist Theological Seminary, I do so without the slightest reservation. Moreover, I am not penning a personal *nihil obstat* with respect to *every* English version. I myself have published criticisms of one or two contemporary translations;[1] and subsequent study and reading have not changed these published opinions, although they may perhaps have altered some individual judgments.

The present slender volume is not an exhaustive treatise. It is not even a rapid survey of modern English translations of the Bible. That sort of book has already been written.[2] Rather, these pages are given over to an easy introduction to two things: biblical textual criticism, that branch of biblical study which examines and correlates the manuscripts from which our English Bibles are translated; and some of the principles upon which translations are made. Moreover, with the possible exception of the appendix, this book aims at being minimally technical. It is designed for students, pastors, and laymen who have no personal knowledge of the primary literature, but who find themselves influenced by the writings of the Trinitarian Bible Society and parallel groups, and do not know where to turn to find a popular rebuttal.

Objections against abandoning the KJV fall into two classes. In the first, it is argued that the manuscripts behind the KJV are more reliable and stand closer to the autographs than does the textual tradition behind virtually all of the Eng-

---

1. E.g., D. A. Carson, "The New English Bible: An Evaluation," *NJT* 1 (1972): 3–14.

2. Cf. Sakae Kubo and Walter Specht, *So Many Versions? Twentieth Century English Versions of the Bible* (Grand Rapids: Zondervan, 1975).

lish versions since 1880. In the second class stand all those miscellaneous arguments that contend for the stylistic superiority of the KJV, or its appropriateness for worship, accuracy of translation, the ease with which it may be memorized, or the like. I shall treat these areas in turn.

PART 1

The Textual Question

CHAPTER 1

The Early Circulation of the New Testament

The invention of the printing press is, arguably, the most significant technical invention since the wheel. When it put in an appearance, not only did it make books much cheaper, circulate knowledge more widely, and contribute largely to the education of the masses, it produced thousands of copies of books and papers that could not be distinguished from one another. The relevance of this latter observation to the present discussion is obvious. Before the printing press, the New Testament (and all other) documents were copied by hand. People are not capable of copying a lengthy piece of written material without introducing some errors. This is easily proved. Sit down and copy out the Gospel of John (from whatever translation you like). After you have finished, read it through and correct it. Then give it to two or three friends and have each of them correct your correction. No more evidence will be needed.

The New Testament documents were copied in several different settings. In the earliest period, manuscripts were copied by Christians either for their own use or for the use of sister churches. People were on the move in the first two centuries, not least Christians; and as they moved, so did their manuscripts. Paul might write a letter to the church in Colossae while sitting under house arrest in Rome (if the imprisonment in question is his first incarceration in Rome, a likely interpretation), but that letter was soon copied by several within the church, and by a few more in the sister church at nearby Laodicea. Perhaps one of the members on a business trip to Macedonia took a copy with him; and while in Philippi he copied out the Letter to the Philippians at the same time someone in the church at Philippi copied out the Letter to the Colossians. Of course any error that the Colossian businessman inadvertently introduced into his own copy of Paul's letter to the Colossians would get picked up by the Philippian copier. Perhaps the Philippian copier knew the Colossian businessman. He recognized him to be a nice man, very devout and godly, but somewhat flamboyant, and judged him to be somewhat careless in scholarly enterprises. The opinion of the Philippian copier might be confirmed if he detected several spelling mistakes in his friend's copy, or if he discovered the Colossian businessman had accidentally put in a word or a line twice, or seemed to have left something out. Without saying anything, he might decide to correct such errors. Unfortunately, because he did not have the autograph at hand by which to correct his own work, he might think he detected an error where there was none! In that case his "correction" was itself an error.

In time, for both good and bad reasons, the church became more institutionalized. Translations of the Greek New Testament were made so people could read God's Word in their own tongue: Syriac, Latin, Coptic (a late form of Egyptian), and so forth. In the fourth century, Augustine complained that everyone who knew a little Greek and who thought he could translate went ahead and did so. By now, too, the New Testament documents were being published professionally. A reader would read each sentence slowly while eight or ten professional scribes made copies.

The textual critic sifts this material and tries to establish, wherever there is doubt, what reading reflects the original or is closest to it. When it is realized that there are approximately five thousand manuscripts of a part or the whole of the Greek

New Testament, in addition to about eight thousand manuscripts of the relevant versions, it is clear that the textual critic has his work cut out for him.

The Greek manuscripts are regularly classified as follows:

1. *Uncials*. This term refers to manuscripts written in capital letters. The copier usually took some pains in his task: the letters had to be more deliberately executed than letters in running script, and the use of this more formal style of handwriting was often reserved for literary works.

2. *Cursive scripts*. Nonliterary, everyday documents such as letters, bills, receipts, deeds, and the like, were written in a cursive or "running" script. Most extant manuscripts of New Testament books are cursives; and most of these are minuscules.

3. *Minuscules*. About the ninth century A.D. a reform in handwriting took place, with the result that a cursive script using smaller letters was adopted for the production of books. This modified form of cursive writing gained almost instantaneous popularity. A person could write this script very quickly; and because the writing was smaller, more could be squeezed onto each page. Both because minuscules are generally later than uncials, and also because they were easier to produce, minuscule copies of the New Testament outnumber uncials more than ten to one.

4. *Papyri*. This word refers to manuscripts made of papyrus instead of animal skin (vellum). In other words, this term sets off a kind of "paper" rather than a style of writing. Papyrus does not stand up as well as vellum, so it is not surprising that relatively few papyrus manuscripts have survived.

5. *Lectionaries*. These are church reading books containing select portions of the Scriptures, to be read on set days according to a liturgical calendar.

There are other sources of information; but these are the most important. In no instance do we possess the autograph; and I suspect it is just as well, for undoubtedly we would make an idol out of it. What we possess is something over 2,100 lectionary manuscripts, more than 2,700 minuscules, just over 260 uncials, and about 80 papyri. To keep things in perspective, however, it is important to remember that the vast majority of these 5,000 or so manuscripts are fragmentary, preserving a few verses or a few books. Only about 50 of these 5,000 contain the entire New Testament, and only one of these 50 is an uncial (viz., ℵ, codex Sinaiticus). Most of the manuscripts, however, do contain the four Gospels.

In comparison with other books written in antiquity, the New Testament is vastly better attested by surviving records than even the best of the alternatives. It is often noted that Homer's *Iliad* is preserved in 457 papyri, 2 uncials, and 188 minuscules. The first six books of the *Annals*, written by the famous Roman governor and historian Tacitus, are found in a single manuscript dating from the ninth century. By contrast, the New Testament, as I have said, is preserved in five thousand Greek manuscripts and eight thousand manuscripts of versions. Yet despite this abundant supply of manuscript evidence, this providential wealth of material sufficient to embarrass the most industrious textual critic, it is a stark fact that no two manuscripts agree in every detail.

What use can be made of the eight thousand manuscripts of versions? Of course they are not as useful as the Greek manuscripts. Because they are themselves translations of a particular Greek manuscript (or of several), they usually cannot help us in deciding if that parent Greek manuscript had this small variation or that. Subtle differences frequently get lost in translation. Nevertheless these versions do witness to larger or unambiguous readings. They can tell us, for example, if a verse or a line was included in the parent Greek manuscript. By this we may be sure that such and such a reading was known by a certain time and place, or else it could not have been translated into the version.

All this sounds alarming. If no two manuscripts agree, how can we know what the Holy Spirit inspired the New Testament authors to write? The matter is, on the face of it, very difficult. All agree that one cannot simply take the oldest manuscripts and trust them, for they may conceivably be very poor copies, while later manuscripts may be good copies of excellent parents that are now lost. For example, a tenth-century minuscule may conceivably be a good copy of an excellent fourth-century uncial, and therefore prove quite superior to a fifth-century uncial. Nor can one trust oneself to the majority reading at any place. It is quite conceivable that a bad manuscript was copied many times, and that a good manuscript was copied scarcely at all.[1] How then are we to arrive at textual decisons?

1. This point is disputed by Wilbur N. Pickering in *The Identity of the New Testament Text* (Nashville: Nelson, 1977); but I discuss his work in the appendix.

CHAPTER 2

Kinds of Errors in New Testament Manuscripts

Before trying to answer the question of how we are to make textual-critical decisions, I must say something about the kinds of errors introduced into the manuscripts by the early scribes. They are usually divided into two types: the unintentional and the intentional.

Unintentional errors are those in which the scribe had no intention of changing anything. He simply made a mistake. If he was copying a manuscript as a professional scribe, writing down what the reader read out to him and to those working with him, he might hear something incorrectly and therefore make a mistake. For example, he might hear *echomen* instead of *echōmen* ("we have" instead of "let us have"), or vice versa (cf. Rom 5:1). The pronunciation of *ou* and *u* was indistinguishable: this explains the variants in Revelation 1:5, where the KJV is based on a text that reads *lousanti* (". . . and *washed* us . . .") whereas many others follow manuscripts that read *lusanti* (". . . and *freed* us . . ."). The pronouns *hēmeis/humeis* (we/you) and their declensional forms were pronounced almost exactly the same way, and therefore give rise to many uncertainties. Did John write I John in order that *our* joy, or *your* joy, may be complete (I John 1:4)?

After the professional scribes had finished transcribing all the readers had read out, a trained corrector read over what the scribe had written and made corrections. Often, therefore, the reading of the first corrector of a manuscript (often in a different color of ink) is correct. But the corrector might miss some mistakes; and he might even introduce some new ones. I have certainly done that at times when marking papers!

Other kinds of unintentional errors are common if the scribe is copying a manuscript by himself; that is, if, instead of listening to a reader, he is using his own eyes to read the parent manuscript. Certain Greek letters in uncial form are readily confused. A very common error is caused by homoeoteleuton, a similar ending of lines or words: a scribe copies what he sees, but when his eyes return to the parent manuscript he accidentally leaves out a bit because his eyes skip down to a place where the same or a similar ending occurs. Alternatively, for an analogous error, he might unthinkingly copy out the same expression or line twice, because his eyes have skipped back up the page. Another common error involves the transposition of words or expressions. Probably this error arises when the scribe retains a whole clause or verse in his memory as he writes it down; and his memory betrays him. It may further betray him by prompting him to substitute a favored synonym for some particular word. Again, the scribe may unwittingly assimilate some passage in one of the Gospels to the parallel in another Gospel that he has all but memorized. Such assimilation is also frequent in certain pairs of epistles, such as Ephesians and Colossians.

Occasionally, honest errors of judgment have led to the introduction of an error. For example, if a scribe accidentally left out a line or a few words, the corrector might put them in the margin. The next scribe who came along and copied this manuscript might reinsert the words into the text at the wrong place. Alternatively, the marginal note may have been a scribe's comment rather than an integral part of the text; but the scribe who copied that manuscript might well have inserted the note into the new copy he was writing, thus adding something to the text of Scripture that should not be there. No malice was involved, no intentional corruption of the text—

just an error of judgment. Some scribes went about their task so mechanically and thoughtlessly as to perpetrate almost unbelievable blunders. In this regard the story of the fourteenth-century minuscule codex 109 is often told. The scribe who produced it obviously obtained his material from a copy that had Luke's genealogy of Jesus (3:23–38) in two columns of twenty-eight lines each. Instead of copying the material in the first column, and then the material in the next column, the scribe followed the lines across the two columns. This has the effect of making almost everyone in the genealogy the son of the wrong father. The list no longer ends with "Adam, the Son of God," for God is now stuck in the middle, appearing as the son of Aram. And the source of the entire race is not God but Phares.[1]

Intentional changes constitute the other class of variants. Although the scribe in these cases *intends* to change what he has in front of him, nevertheless it must be observed that in the vast majority of instances he changes something he thinks is wrong. By "wrong" I do not mean that the scribe feels he knows more than God; rather, in most instances he changes things that he thinks the preceding scribe has corrupted. Sometimes too scribes tried to improve on grammar, vocabulary, and spelling, preferring the literary Attic Greek of an earlier era to the colloquial Hellenistic Greek (the so-called Koine) in which the New Testament had been written.

Another kind of intentional corruption came about by the desire, conscious or not, to harmonize one account with

---

1. This and other causes of error are discussed in what is still the best introduction to textual criticism, Bruce M. Metzger, *The Text of the New Testament: Its Transmission, Corruption, and Restoration,* 2d ed. (New York: Oxford University, 1968), pp. 186ff. Other standard works designed to introduce the student to textual criticism include: F. G. Kenyon, *The Text of the Greek Bible,* 3d ed., rev. A. W. Adams (London: Duckworth, 1975); J. Harold Greenlee, *Introduction to New Testament Textual Criticism* (Grand Rapids: Eerdmans, 1964), a volume written by an evangelical; Vincent Taylor, *The Text of the New Testament: A Short Introduction,* 2d ed. (London: Macmillan, 1963); Jack Finegan, *Encountering New Testament Manuscripts: A Working Introduction to Textual Criticism* (Grand Rapids: Eerdmans, 1974), a most attractive volume, though not as full a discussion as that of Metzger. Cf. also *The Cambridge History of the Bible,* 3 vols. (London: Cambridge University, 1963–1970).

another. Every reader of the Gospels, for example, is familiar with the fact that parallel pericopae[2] may not include precisely the same information. The manuscript tradition bears ample witness to the zeal displayed by some copyists in smoothing over such divergences. Again, many phrases have natural complements. If I say, "the scribes," some will think immediately of the complementary adjunct, "and the Pharisees"; and, sure enough, some copyists added such complements, wittingly or otherwise. Again, a scribe sometimes had several manuscripts in front of him when he made his copy. If he discovered that one manuscript had one reading, and a second another, he either chose one and left the other, or he put the two together to make a conflated reading. If some manuscripts preserve the reading "church of God" in Acts 20:28, and others preserve "church of the Lord," some later copyists conflate the two to produce "church of the Lord and God," providing their readers with the benefit of both readings.

Some intentional changes were introduced because of doctrinal considerations. The most famous example, of course, is the canon of Marcion. During the second century Marcion removed all references to Jesus' Jewish background. Tatian's *Diatessaron* alters the text in several places in order to support ascetic values. Quite a number of such changes have been detected.

Before taking the discussion further, I should pause and set at rest the troubled concern of anyone who, on the basis of what I have written so far, concludes that the manuscript tradition is entirely unreliable, or that we can not really be *certain* of any of it. There is no need for such rigorous pessimism. The vast majority of the manuscript errors have to do with details of orthography, word order, and the like. Moreover, many of the theologically significant variants can be sorted out quite easily by comparing manuscript with manuscript. The result, as I shall try to show, is a certain word from God.

2. A pericope (*pl.* pericopae) is the technical name for a section, an individual unit, of the Gospels.

24

CHAPTER 3

Text-Types

The aim of the textual critic is to ascertain, as precisely as possible, what reading of any particular passage is closest to the original, or accurately reflects the original. The first step is to classify the manuscript evidence in such a way as to make it manageable. As the church became more institutionalized, certain definable manuscript traditions tended to become the standards within more or less defined areas. To take an example from the Latin versions, by the end of the fourth century there were many Latin translations of the New Testament, most of inferior quality. In 382, Damasus, bishop of Rome,[1] secured the services of Jerome to produce the best Latin translation possible, which would then be the "official" one. Jerome's work became the forerunner of the modern Vulgate. Damasus, of course, was wise in his policy. By his time relatively few people in the western Mediterranean world could read Greek, and Jerome's work (which, interestingly, suffered a great deal of criticism and flak before it was well-nigh univer-

---

1. He is regularly referred to as "pope"; but although the Roman see held pride of place in the West in the fourth century, the bishop who occupied that see enjoyed little of the splendor and authority now associated with the title "pope."

25

sally accepted in the Western church), added stability and consistency to a situation that had become intolerable.

The Greek manuscripts of the New Testament are generally grouped together into "text-types." This means that the manuscripts belonging to a particular text-type all reflect the same sort of errors, the same variants at crucial passages, the same general pattern of development. Of course, because all of the manuscripts in any one text-type have themselves been hand-copied, no two manuscripts in any one textual tradition are *precisely* identical. Nevertheless a manuscript can often be assigned to one text-type or another; and if a manuscript reflects two or more text-types, it is said to be mixed.

The most common general classification of text-types is summarized in the following paragraphs; but I should point out that research continues, and the classification may prove somewhat idealized. A greater number of early manuscripts boast a mixed text than has often been thought. Yet, although this classification may be idealized, the extremes of the various textual traditions have been isolated, and the only question is whether these extremes achieve a sufficiently broad early following to be graced with the expression "text-type." Such details do not affect my argument at this point. They are dealt with at somewhat greater length in the appendix.

1. *The Byzantine text*. This is the textual tradition which, in large measure, stands behind the KJV. It was largely preserved in the Byzantine Empire, which continued to use Greek, unlike the (western) Roman Empire and its offshoots, for which Latin was the common language. There are far more manuscripts extant in this tradition than in the other three combined; but on the other hand, most of these manuscript witnesses are relatively late.

2. *The Western text*. There is considerable scholarly dispute about this text-type. Some scholars hold that the Western text is the creation of a group of scribes whose work developed in more rather than less confusion as each generation of scribes toiled without knowledge and care. A few contend for an individual scribe at the heart of the tradition. Others argue that the text-type is not homogeneous enough to be considered a true textual recension, and postulate that the manuscripts

classified under the "Western" rubric sprang from fairly wild and undisciplined scribal activity.

3. *The Caesarean text.* This text-type probably originated in Egypt and may have been brought to Caesarea by Origen. It boasts a unique mixture of Western (above) and Alexandrian (below) readings, prompting some scholars to question the value of calling it a text-type.

4. *The Alexandrian text.* This text-type was probably prepared by trained scribes, most likely in Alexandria and its regions. F. J. A. Hort called its prime exemplars the "Neutral" text and ascribed to them a preeminence that has been somewhat mitigated by subsequent research. Nevertheless the Alexandrian text has excellent credentials, far better than its harshest critics have been willing to concede. On this I shall have more to say.

CHAPTER 4

Some Criteria for Making Textual Choices

Before turning to the nub of the debate, I propose now to sketch in some of the criteria scholars use to determine what reading is most likely closest to the original. The evidence may conveniently be divided into two sorts, the external and the internal.

The external evidence includes the date of a particular manuscript witness, the geographical distribution of the witnesses that agree on a reading, and the genealogical relationship of the witness to the text-types. None of these considerations is considered decisive; all have to be weighed. Other things being equal, an older document may be more authoritative than a more recent one. But the date of the text-type is more important than the date of a particular witness. For example, if it can be established that at the close of the second century Irenaeus used a text-type found in a tenth-century minuscule, that minuscule will be considered more important than a fifth-century uncial whose text-type cannot be traced back further than the fourth century. Geographical distribution is also important, for if a particular reading is found in several widely separated areas, it is correspondingly less likely to be the idiosyncratic error of a geographically contained region. The relationship of the witnesses to the text-types is extremely important, because if all the witnesses that support a particular reading are from one text-type, then they may all be copies of copies of copies that spring from one manuscript. Manuscripts must therefore be weighed, and not just counted. Of course, if all those manuscripts came from one textual tradition, that tradition *may* in fact preserve the original reading; but this cannot be presumed from the number of manuscript witnesses per se. If the other three types agree on *another* reading, even though they collectively embrace a smaller number of actual manuscripts, then it is in principle more likely that they preserve the original reading, other things being equal.

The internal evidence involves a consideration of several probabilities. I shall not take the time to list all of these; but I must offer three or four. *In general,* the shorter reading is to be preferred, since it is demonstrable that later scribes, at least, tended to add bits rather than remove them.[1] There are, of course, many exceptions. If something has been omitted because of homoeoteleuton, or because the scribe has apparently judged something to be irreverent, superfluous, or contrary to ascetic practice or current pious belief, then the longer reading is to be preferred. Again, in general the most difficult reading (that is, more difficult to the scribe) is to be preferred, since a scribe is more likely to emend a difficult reading than an easy one. What we are considering here is transcriptional probability. One must also take into account what the original human author was more likely to have written. For example, there is a distinctive Pauline vocabulary and a peculiar Johannine style; and sometimes it is possible to make an educated guess from among three or four variants on the basis of what the author does elsewhere. None of these probabilities is, of course, decisive. If they all line up one particular way, we may be very certain indeed. However, sometimes the strength of two of these probabilities cancels each other out. For example, the probability that a particular reading in Romans is original because Paul elsewhere expresses himself that way, may have to

1. Again, the appendix provides a little more discussion about scribal habits and the use sometimes made of the work of A. C. Clark, who argued that ancient scribes tended to drop things out rather than add them in.

be set over against the probability that copying scribes would be more likely to convert a non-Pauline locution into a Pauline one rather than vice versa. In weighing these things, the textual critic will look for the reading that best explains the genesis of all the other variants.

I have not included chapter-and-verse examples of text-critical problems: these can be found in any of the books on the subject. I have aimed at conveying in capsule form a little of how difficult and painstaking the work of the textual critic must be. Nevertheless, the vast majority of the lines of the Greek New Testament may be regarded as textually certain. A number of others are certain to a high degree of probability. A relative handful constitute famous problems that are debated constantly in books and in journal literature.[2]

---

2. For example, cf. René Kieffer, "'Afin que je sois brûlé' ou bien 'Afin que j'en tire orgueil'? (I Cor. xiii. 3)," *NTS* 22 (1975): 95-97; or the magisterial study by Kurt Aland, "Eine Untersuchung zu Joh 1:3-4: Über die Bedeutung eines Punktes," *ZNW* 59 (1968): 174-209.

CHAPTER 5

Origins of
the Textus Receptus

To do preliminary text-critical work on the New
Testament it is sufficient to use several of the printed critical
editions of the New Testament.[1] For serious detailed study it is
essential to use at least the printed photographs and transcriptions of the actual manuscripts, and preferable to spend some
time on the manuscripts themselves.

The first edition of the Greek New Testament to be published (though not the first to be printed)[2] was edited by the

1. Probably the most widely used critical editions of the Greek New Testament are: (1) *Hē Kainē Diathēkē,* ed. Erwin Nestle and G. D. Kilpatrick, 2d
ed. (London: British and Foreign Bible Society, 1958); (2) *The Greek New
Testament,* ed. Kurt Aland, Matthew Black, Carlo M. Martini, Bruce M.
Metzger, and Allen Wikgren, 3d ed. (London: United Bible Societies, 1975);
and (3) *Novum Testamentum Graece,* ed. Eberhard Nestle, Erwin Nestle,
and Kurt Aland, 25th ed. (London: United Bible Societies, 1963). This last
one is by far the best in that it provides best evidence for most variants; but its
critical apparatus is fairly complicated and presupposes a working knowledge
of textual traditions.

2. The first Greek New Testament to be printed came off the press in 1514.
It was part of a polyglot Bible (Hebrew, Aramaic, Greek, and Latin), the
brainchild of the Roman Catholic cardinal primate of Spain, Francisco
Ximenes de Cisneros (1437-1517), although it was executed by several
scholars. Printed in the university town of Alcala, which was called Complu-

Dutch scholar Desiderius Erasmus (1469-1536) of Rotterdam, Holland. The work, published in March 1516, was done somewhat precipitately, with the result that there are countless hundreds of printing errors. To prepare his text Erasmus utilized several Greek manuscripts, not one of which contained the entire New Testament. None of his manuscripts was earlier than the twelfth century. For the Book of Revelation he had but one manuscript, and it was lacking the final leaf, which contained the last six verses of the book. Therefore Erasmus translated the Latin Vulgate back into Greek and published that. Hence in the last six verses of Revelation in Erasmus's Greek New Testament, several words and phrases may be found that are attested in no Greek manuscript whatsoever.[3] Even in a few other places in the New Testament, Erasmus introduced material from the Vulgate. For example, in Acts 9:6 the words, "And he trembling and astonished said, Lord, what wilt thou have me to do?" (KJV) are found in no Greek manuscript at all. They are an obvious assimilation to the parallel account in Acts 22:10.

Erasmus's second edition was, like the first, a diglot; that is, it is in two languages, Greek and Erasmus's own rather elegant Latin translation, a translation that differed considerably from the generally accepted Vulgate. This second edition became the basis of Luther's German translation.

Not all scholars were pleased with Erasmus's work. Many thought Erasmus's Latin translation a presumptuous attack on the venerated Vulgate. Erasmus had also provided some annotations justifying his translation, and these annotations included sharp barbs aimed at the corrupt Roman Catholic clergy. On a number of fronts, therefore, Erasmus had left himself open to attack.

One attack concerned his omission of the trinitarian formula in I John 5:7-8: ". . . the Father, the Word, and the

---

tum in Latin, this Bible came to be known as the Complutensian Polyglot. It was not put on the open market, and therefore the edition of Desiderius Erasmus receives credit for being the first *published* Greek New Testament.

3. For the details, cf. Bruce M. Metzger, *The Text of the New Testament: Its Transmission, Corruption, and Restoration*, 2d ed. (New York: Oxford University, 1968), p. 100 (n. 1).

Holy Ghost: and these three are one. And there are three that bear witness in earth. . . ." Erasmus answered the charges by observing reasonably enough the he had not found the words in any Greek manuscript, including several he had examined subsequent to publishing his material. Let Bruce M. Metzger take up the story:

> In an unguarded moment Erasmus promised that he would insert the *Comma Johanneum,* as it is called, in future editions if a single Greek manuscript could be found that contained the passage. At length such a copy was found — or was made to order! As it now appears, the Greek manuscript had probably been written in Oxford about 1520 [a year after the publication of the second edition] by a Franciscan friar named Froy (or Roy), who took the disputed words from the Latin Vulgate. Erasmus stood by his promise and inserted the passage in his third edition (1522), but he indicates in a lengthy footnote his suspicions that the manuscript had been prepared expressly in order to confute him.[4]

The manuscript in question is codex minuscule 61, now in the library of Trinity College, Dublin. Among the thousands of other Greek manuscripts that have come to light since this episode in the life of Erasmus, only three others attest to the reading. One is minuscule 88, a twelfth-century manuscript with the relevant words scribbled onto the margin in a seventeenth-century hand; a sixteenth-century copy of the Complutensian Polyglot Greek text, which was also under the influence of the Vulgate; and one other manuscript that is variously dated to the fourteenth or seventeenth century. However, the *Comma Johanneum* is cited in a fourth-century Latin treatise usually attributed to Priscillian. It probably sprang from allegorical exegesis of the three witnesses and, written on an early margin of a Latin manuscript of I John, became an established gloss in the Old Latin Bible in the fifth century. It appears in no copy of the Latin Vulgate before about A.D. 800.

Although Erasmus published a fourth and fifth edition, we need say no more about them here. Erasmus's Greek Testament stands in line behind the King James Version; yet it rests

---

4. Ibid., p. 101.

upon a half dozen minuscule manuscripts, none of which is earlier than the tenth century. It was later reprinted by various publishers, the most important of whom was the Parisian Robert Estienne (his surname was regularly Latinized as Stephanus). He issued four editions of the Greek Testament. His third (dated 1550) is the first critical edition: Stephanus referred in the margins to the readings from fourteen codices and from the Complutensian Polyglot. His first two editions (dated 1546 and 1549, respectively) are largely a compound of the Complutensian Polyglot and Erasmus's editions. In his third edition, however, Stephanus leaned more heavily on Erasmus, especially on Erasmus's fourth and fifth editions. In his fourth edition (1551), Stephanus divided up the text into numbered verses. Theodore Beza, successor of John Calvin and front-rank classical and biblical scholar, published a further nine editions of the Greek New Testament; but the text that he used differs but little from that of Stephanus's fourth edition of 1551. The translators of the King James Version relied largely on Beza's editions of 1588–1589 and 1598.

In 1624, thirteen years after the publication of the KJV, the Elzevir brothers, Bonaventure and Abraham, published a compact Greek New Testament, the text of which was largely that of Beza. In the second edition, published in 1633, there is an advertising blurb (Metzger's term) that says, in Latin, "Textum ergo habes, nunc ab omnibus receptum: in quo nihil immutatem aut corruptum damus" ("The text that you have is now received by all, in which we give nothing changed or perverted"). This is the origin of the term *Textus Receptus* (or TR, as it is often referred to): the Latin words *"textum . . . receptum"* have simply been put into the nominative. The TR is not the "received text" in the sense that it has been received from God *as over against* other Greek manuscripts. Rather, it is the "received text" in the sense that it was the standard one at the time of the Elzevirs. Nevertheless the textual basis of the TR is a small number of haphazardly collected and relatively late minuscule manuscripts. In about a dozen places its reading is attested by no known Greek manuscript witness.

The TR, or minor modifications of it, became the basis of every European translation until 1881. The dominant manuscripts of the TR were taken from the Byzantine tradition. True, Stephanus had access to D (codex Bezae), the best exemplar of the Western text-type; but it was sufficiently different from his other witnesses that he made little use of it. Thus the Byzantine tradition reigned supreme for more than two centuries.

To keep a correct perspective it is important to note that the TR is not exactly the same as the Byzantine tradition. The Byzantine text-type is found in several thousand witnesses, while the TR did not refer to one hundredth of that evidence.

CHAPTER 6

Modern Defense of the Byzantine Text-Type

This brings us to the heart of the contemporary dispute over textual matters. A small number of very vocal evangelicals argue strongly, in books and pamphlets, that the TR, and therefore the KJV, better preserves the original text than any other text-type. Modern English versions, without exception, are based either on a different text-type or on an eclectic text, in which the translators follow no text-type slavishly but examine each reading on its own individual merits. This procedure is called "eclecticism."

The best known of the evangelical defenders of the TR are Terence Brown of the Trinitarian Bible Society; David Otis Fuller, editor of several books, including *Which Bible?* and *True or False?;*[1] Zane C. Hodges of Dallas Theological Seminary (although I understand he does not represent an official view at Dallas); and Edward F. Hills, author of, among other things, *Believing Bible Study;*[2] and one or two more-recent

---

1. *Which Bible?* (Grand Rapids: Grand Rapids International Publications, 1970); *True or False? The Westcott-Hort Theory Examined* (Grand Rapids: Grand Rapids International Publications, 1973).

2. *Believing Bible Study* (Des Moines: Christian Research, 1967).

writers.[3] In addition to these men, a larger number of writers have written pamphlets, tracts, and short books popularizing their viewpoint.

I shall try to sum up the position of these men as fairly as I can. Not all of them stress all of the points I am about to outline; but I think each would concur with most of them, if not quite all.

In the opinion of the defenders of the TR, the textual-critical theories advanced by B. F. Westcott and F. J. A. Hort toward the end of the last century are both bad theology and bad textual criticism. Westcott and Hort, who had at their disposal the newly discovered codex Sinaiticus and, by 1889–1890, the newly published codex Vaticanus, along with many other manuscripts of various dates, followed the lead of J. A. Bengel in recognizing the importance of text-types over against individual manuscripts per se. They argued that the Byzantine textual tradition (which includes the TR) did not originate before the mid-fourth century, and that it was the result of a conflation of earlier texts. This text was taken to Constantinople, where it became popular, spreading throughout the Byzantine Empire. This text-type, which I have designated Byzantine, Hort referred to as Syrian. Because, in their view, it was a conflation of the Western and Alexandrian texts, it is the fullest; but for the same reason it is the furthest re-

---

3. By far the most influential of these books is *Which Bible?*, which has gone through a half dozen editions (the one cited throughout this book is the 5th ed., 1975). Perhaps the most influential person among the defenders of the KJV is Terence Brown, secretary of the Trinitarian Bible Society. His many tracts and pamphlets, as well as the TBS's *Quarterly Record*, have circulated widely. TBS has also recently reprinted F. H. A. Scrivener's Greek New Testament, essentially the TR. The nineteenth-century critic John W. Burgon also enjoys wide popularity among the defenders of the TR. Some of his work has been reprinted, the most important being *The Last Twelve Verses of the Gospel According to S. Mark* (Ann Arbor, Mich.: Sovereign Grace Book Club, 1959), which contains an extensive introduction by Edward F. Hills. The most erudite defender of the Byzantine tradition is probably Jakob van Bruggen, author of the recently published book, *The Ancient Text of the New Testament*, trans. C. Kleijn (Winnipeg: Premier, 1976). A still more recent defender of the Byzantine tradition is Wilbur N. Pickering, author of *The Identity of the New Testament Text* (Nashville: Nelson, 1977). His work, in my view, is more significant than that of most of his colleagues, and so I have treated it separately in the appendix to this book.

moved from the autographs. Westcott and Hort gave much weight to the Alexandrian tradition; but preeminent emphasis was laid on B and ℵ (Vaticanus and Sinaiticus), considered to be a parallel development of the Alexandrian tradition and designated by them the "Neutral text." Subsequent textual-critical work accepted the theories of Westcott and Hort, although with modifications. For example, today B and ℵ are seen to be part of the Alexandrian text-type, and few refer to this text-type as "Neutral." But almost universally accepted today is the contention of Westcott and Hort that the Byzantine tradition does not antedate the middle of the fourth century and represents a relatively late conflation. It is on this basis that Bible translations since 1881 have, *as compared with the KJV*, left out some things and added a few others.

Westcott and Hort, therefore, are the chief culprits as far as the defenders are concerned. These defenders claim that the Byzantine tradition stands closer to the original than does any other text-type; that the other text-types were rejected by the early church; that the reason the other texts are shorter is that they *omitted* material from a Byzantine type of text; that such omissions were often prompted by heretical beliefs such as Arianism, which denied the deity of Christ; that the uncials B and ℵ (for examples) are not only fourth-century manuscripts, but represent a text-type that only originated in the fourth century, under the influence of heretical conditions and careless scholarship; that the Byzantine tradition, which boasts the majority of the manuscripts, thus boasts heavy manuscript evidence that must not be ignored; that the fact that the church used the Byzantine tradition from *at least* the fourth to the nineteenth century argues irrefutably for the providential care of God over that traditon; that Westcott and Hort were heretics whose modernistic bias prevented them from exercising objective analysis of the evidence; that all modern versions based on non-Byzantine text-types are in fact denying the verbal inspiration of Scripture by omitting parts of God's Word; that the reason no Greek manuscripts of the Byzantine tradition antedate about A.D. 400 (a point that on the face of it obviously favors Westcott and Hort) is that such manuscripts were in constant use and therefore wore out; that the theory of

Westcott and Hort concerning the genesis of the Byzantine text-type involves unacceptable circular reasoning; that the real genesis of the Byzantine tradition is so obscure, not because of its being a late conflation, but because of its primitive origin; that the Alexandrian text is a particularly notorious *revision* of a Byzantine type of text; that the Byzantine text could not have been a conflation of other texts because scribes did not use desks to write on, and without a place to lay down the manuscripts, scribes could not possibly have engaged in systematic conflation; that what the majority of believers in the history of the church have believed to be true is true, and that this principle supports the preeminence of the Byzantine tradition.

This theory is being presented in popular literature to pastors and laymen everywhere, many of whom have never read a rebuttal at the same level and who are not equipped to do the more advanced work that demonstrates the theory to be false. Moreover, because the defenders of the TR associate this theory with a high view of Scripture, fellow evangelicals with an equally high view of Scripture are often a little nervous about speaking out, for fear they will come under suspicion by their peers. As more of this pro-TR literature comes rolling off the press, more and more Christians are being caught up in the debate.

CHAPTER 7

Fourteen Theses

In what follows I shall not argue that the vociferous defenders of the TR are knaves or fools. I shall seek to demonstrate, rather, that their interpretation of the evidence is mistaken. Moreover I shall point out logical fallacies in their exposition and the alarming way in which they cite arguments in their own favor without examining those arguments. Their presuppositions in favor of the TR have made most of them careless about determining the truth of many of their oft-repeated contentions, with the result that not only their interpretation of the facts is incorrect, but also their alleged "facts" are far too often simply untrue. Moreover the pamphleteers, most of them concerned pastors who believe the abandonment of the KJV to be a sign of the corruption and degeneracy of the age, cite the few seminal works of Terence Brown, Zane C. Hodges, Edward F. Hills, and their nineteenth-century fellow protagonist John W. Burgon, as if every line they have written is true; and not lacking in zeal but lacking in firsthand knowledge of the data and of the first-class textual work done by men like Benjamin B. Warfield, J. Gresham Machen, and in our own day Gordon D. Fee—all conservatives who are convinced that the Byzantine text-type is late—they repeat the errors of their mentors with multiplying fervor. For these reasons the beginnings of major strife and division are brewing quietly in several conservative denominations scattered throughout countries of the English-speaking world.

I shall proceed by stating and briefly defending fourteen theses.

Thesis 1: *There is no unambiguous evidence that the Byzantine text-type was known before the middle of the fourth century.* This point may be established by: (1) determining if there are any Greek manuscripts of pre–A.D. 350 date which reflect the Byzantine text-type; (2) examining pre–A.D. 350 versions for the same information; (3) reading the New Testament quotations found in the writings of the pre–A.D. 350 church fathers to discover if the biblical passages they quote approximate any particular text-type. In each case the evidence is uniform: the mature Byzantine text-type appears nowhere before the fourth century.

I do not deny that readings found in the Byzantine text-type are found in the ante-Nicene period; but almost all of these readings are also found in other text-types (mostly Western). In any case the early existence of a text-type can be established not merely by appeal to numbers of readings, but only by appeal to numbers of readings in conjunction with discrete patterns of readings. Discrete readings that are Byzantine *and* something else offer, at best, ambiguous evidence.[1]

It has not been proved conclusively that the Byzantine text-type did *not* exist before the fourth century. However, although there is not unambiguous historical evidence that it existed before the fourth century, there is clear historical evidence that the other three textual traditions do stretch back to this ante-Nicene period: on this latter point I shall have more to say a little further on.

The theory advanced by B. F. Westcott and F. J. A. Hort to account for these facts is that the Byzantine text was formed

---

1. This too is discussed with a trifle more technical detail in the appendix. On the way Origen cites Scripture, see the important article by Gordon D. Fee, "The Text of John in Origen and Cyril of Alexandria: A Contribution to Methodology in the Recovery and Analysis of Patristic Citations," *Bib* 52 (1971): 357–94.

as a conflation between A.D. 250 and 350. The theory is a reasonable way of accounting for the appearance in history of this text-type about A.D. 350; but it is also reasonable, as we shall see, because of the internal character of the Byzantine textual tradition (see thesis 3, below). Nevertheless I am not arguing for the details of the Westcott and Hort theory; I am merely saying the advocates of the primacy of the Byzantine text-type must account for the historical data. There are many volumes of writings by the ante-Nicene fathers, and not one of them unambiguously reflects the Byzantine textual tradition: and it is essential that such data be accounted for.

There are two common replies made by the defenders of the TR at this point. The first concerns the Peshitta Syriac version of the New Testament, and it is found in a publication of the Trinitarian Bible Society:[2]

> In his book on the N. T. Canon (1855), Westcott himself saw "no reason to desert the opinion which has obtained the sanction of the most competent scholars, that the formation of the Peshitto Syriac was to be fixed within the first half of the 2nd century. The very obscurity which hangs over its origin is *proof* (the italics do not belong to Westcott!) of its venerable age, because it shows that it grew up spontaneously among Christian congregations. . . . Had it been a work of later date, of the 3rd or 4th century, it is scarcely possible that its history should be so uncertain as it is." In the "Introduction to the N.T. in Greek," 1882, Westcott contradicted himself on all these points and contended that the Curetonian Syriac was of greater antiquity, and that the Peshitto was an authoritative revision in the latter part of the 3rd or 4th centuries.

Several comments are in order. (1) The expression "contradicted himself" is loaded. In fact, almost thirty years' worth of textual research prompted Westcott to change his mind. He is a fool who does not change his mind to conform to truth. (2) In 1885 the Syriac manuscripts available for comparison were much more severely limited than they were later. (3) "Because

---

2. "The Divine Original," p. 7. The point is frequently discussed: e.g., cf. Edward F. Hills's introduction to John W. Burgon, *The Last Twelve Verses of the Gospel According to S. Mark* (Ann Arbor, Mich.: Sovereign Grace Book Club, 1959), pp. 55–57.

the Peshitta was accepted as the standard version of the Scriptures by both Eastern and Western branches of Syrian Christendom, one must conclude that it had attained some degree of status prior to the split in the Syrian church in A.D. 431."[3] This establishes a terminus ad quem for the Peshitta; it does not establish when the work was done. (4) The Curetonian Syriac manuscript, one of two that makes up the "Old Syriac" tradition, was published in 1858, three years after Westcott's 1855 volume; and the other manuscript that makes up this tradition, a palimpsest designated syr^{sin}, was not even discovered until 1892. (5) In fact, five different Syriac versions of all or part of the New Testament have now been identified. (6) Of the 350 or so manuscripts of the Peshitta version, a few go back to the fifth or sixth centuries: none earlier. (7) The text behind it appears to be mixed, although as far as I know, exhaustive work has been done on only some parts of it. Apparently the Gospels in the Peshitta reflect a Byzantine tradition, whereas Acts offers agreements with the Western text. This *may* indicate that various hands worked on the Peshitta at different times. (8) In any case, I know of only one who reads Syriac competently who dates the Peshitta before about A.D. 400.[4] (9) However, if we may *suppose* (against the evidence) that the Peshitta did exist about A.D. 200, and that it boasts enough textual affinities to the Byzantine text-type to suggest the latter were already well established, what would be entailed? It would mean that the Byzantine text-type is as early as the other three text-types; but it would *not necessarily* mean that the Byzantine text stands closer to the original.

In fact, not all defenders of the TR argue for an early date for the Peshitta. It is more common instead to resort to a

3. Bruce M. Metzger, *The Text of the New Testament: Its Transmission, Corruption, and Restoration,* 2d ed. (New York: Oxford University, 1968), p. 70.

4. I do not count myself as "one who reads Syriac competently." I can slowly and painfully pick my way through a printed Syriac text; but I would be loath to grace this process with the word *reading*. The scholar to whom I refer is Arthur Vööbus, who in 1947 criticized the work of F. C. Burkitt, the scholar who had demonstrated the lateness of the Peshitta. Vööbus himself, however, was decisively answered by Matthew Black, "Rabbula of Edessa and the Peshitta," *BJRL* 33 (1950-51): 203-10.

second argument to account for the absence of evidence for a pre–A.D. 350 Byzantine text-type. Repeatedly it is claimed that the reason why there are no exemplars of a Byzantine text-type before the mid-fourth century is that they all wore out from much use. These were the manuscripts, it is argued, that were copied again and again, and therefore they quickly became tattered and had to be thrown out. The early manuscripts that we do possess, and that reflect non-Byzantine text-types, were, according to this theory, quickly rejected by the early church as inferior and therefore not handled so much. It is for this reason they they have been preserved.

This ingenious theory is quite untenable for at least the following reasons: (1) Although it may explain why the autographs disappeared, it cannot explain why there are *no* extant copies of manuscripts with Byzantine text-type from before the fourth century. If such manuscripts were handled *and copied* so much that they wore out, then many copies must have been made. Why have *none* of them survived? (2) The ante-Nicene fathers unambiguously cited every text-type *except* the Byzantine. Therefore defenders of the "worn-out manuscripts" hypothesis must not only base this hypothesis on an argument from silence (there are no early manuscripts with Byzantine text-type), but also pit it against the hard data that the early fathers never unambiguously cited from it. Is it not eminently more reasonable to conclude that manuscripts with Byzantine text simply did not exist for the first 250–300 years of the church's life? (3) If they did exist, who was wearing them out? If the fathers did not cite the Byzantine text-type, who then was handling these alleged manuscripts so frequently and thoughtlessly that they wore out?[5]

5. Hills has advanced a modified form of this theory, recently taken up by David Otis Fuller in the opening chapter, "Why This Book?," of *Which Bible?*, 5th ed. (Grand Rapids: Grand Rapids International Publications, 1975). Because it has been very difficult to find many precise cases of direct copying (the Ferrar group of manuscripts being a notable exception), Hills picks up on a suggestion made by Kirsopp Lake: it was common practice for the parent manuscript to be destroyed after the copies had been made and checked. This, argue Hills and Fuller, could account for the absence of early Byzantine manuscripts: they were used as exemplars to be copied and were consequently destroyed. The answers to this ingenious theory are obvious:

Thesis 2: *The argument that defends the Byzantine tradition by appealing to the fact that most extant manuscripts of the Greek New Testament attest to this Byzantine text-type, is logically fallacious and historically naive.* Hodges, for example, in his article in *Which Bible?*, seems to regard it as a truism that the majority of the manuscripts in the transmission of any ancient book will, a priori, preserve the best text.[6] But it is not a truism at all. It is quite possible to conceive that the best manuscripts of the New Testament were removed to some relatively quiet corner of the Mediterranean world while inferior manuscripts dominated in publishing centers. Hodges is simply incorrect in supposing his point is a *truism.*[7] The only reply he could possibly venture, I think, is the appeal to providence, on which I shall have more to say.

---

(1) If only one copy were made before the exemplar was destroyed, there would never be more than one extant copy of the Greek New Testament! (2) If several copies were made from one exemplar, then either (a) they were not all made at the same time, and therefore the destruction of the exemplar was not a common practice after all; or (b) they were all made at the same time. (3) If the latter obtains, then it should be possible to identify their sibling relationship; yet in fact such identification is as difficult and as precarious as the identification of direct exemplar/copy manuscripts. This probably means we have lost a lot of manuscripts; and/or it means that the divergences between copy and exemplar, as between copy and sibling copy, are frequently difficult to detect. (4) Why are there *no* copies of the Byzantine text before about A.D. 350, and *so many* from there on? This anomaly, it might be argued, demonstrates that the practice of destroying the exemplar died out during the fourth century. However, neither Hills nor Fuller has argued this, as far as I know, perhaps because they realize Lake did most of his comparative study in this regard on post-fourth-century manuscripts! (5) It needs to be emphasized that the appeal to Lake's suggestion is not an appeal to established fact. It is far from certain that exemplars were destroyed; and if they were, it is indeed certain that they were not always destroyed. (6) In any case this sort of argument does not explain the absence of clear Byzantine citations in the ante-Nicene fathers, nor the absence of early versional evidence supporting the Byzantine text-type. Jakob van Bruggen argues that ninth-century minuscules were based on early Byzantine manuscripts that were then destroyed. *The Ancient Text of the New Testament,* trans. C. Kleijn (Winnipeg: Premier, 1976), pp. 26–27. This is a hypothesis built on silence, and it cannot bear the weight he rests on it.

6. "The Greek Text of the King James Version," in *Which Bible?*, ed. David Otis Fuller, pp. 25–38.

7. Wilbur N. Pickering develops the same sort of argument on a statistical basis in the third appendix of *The Identity of the New Testament Text*

Hodges contends that because most of the early manuscript discoveries, all of non-Byzantine text-type, have come from Egypt, therefore they probably represent a textual tradition pertaining only to that geographical area. The dry climate of Egypt provides the geographical accident that resulted in the discovery of precisely those manuscripts, since manuscripts are least likely to decompose in such an environment.

However, as I have said in thesis 2, this entire reconstruction is both logically fallacious and historically naive. (1) The number of manuscripts that support a reading is not nearly as important as the number of text-types. A particular text-type could, in theory, have three thousand members genealogically related; but ultimately it would still have only one ancestor or conceivably a small handful of ancestors. Another text-type might boast a mere fifty manuscript members; but it too would still have only one ancestor, or conceivably a small handful of ancestors. I can think of no truism, no axiomatic reason, that will dictate that the text-type closest to the original must predominate in number. (2) Although most early non-Byzantine manuscripts have been found in Egypt, it is naive to postulate that the textual tradition they represent is restricted to that area. It is naive not only because not *all* such manuscripts come from Egypt, but more importantly because the early fathers quoted from the text-types represented by those manuscripts, and these early fathers did not all live in Egypt! Moreover the early versions reflect the same text-types, and they too represent wide geographical distribution. (3) If it be true that the hot dry climate of Egypt is something of a geographical accident—and of course, that much is true—it is equally true that the context in which the Byzantine textual tradition was preserved is equally an historical accident. The only major area where Greek was spoken as a living language from about the end of the third century on, was the eastern part of the empire, which came to be known as the Byzantine Empire. The area was further reduced in size by the rise in Islam. It is

---

(Nashville: Nelson, 1977). But his model is utterly dependent on what he calls "normal transmission," and (as I shall later show) it is insensitive to a number of historical facts.

not surprising that the Byzantine textual tradition should predominate: in Byzantium, Greek was still the lingua franca and therefore many Greek copies of the New Testament were needed. In the West the Latin versions took over fairly early; and at the height of the Middle Ages, Greek was scarcely known. With the fall of Constantinople (A.D. 1453), the Byzantine Empire, or what was left of it, collapsed, and many of its scholars fled west, bringing their manuscripts with them. The Renaissance more or less coincided with their arrival; and the new thirst for knowledge, including knowledge of the languages in which the Scriptures had been given, gave impetus to the Reformation and to the early textual work of Desiderius Erasmus. If it be true that about 95 percent of the manuscripts belong to the Byzantine tradition (and it is), it is also true that approximately the same percentage date from periods after the seventh century, when the *Heimat* of Greek had been reduced, more or less, to the Byzantine area.

An important point to remember is that text-types tended to freeze into more rigid forms as the church became more institutionalized. The earlier the period, the more fluid the situation was, partly because the New Testament documents were being copied and circulated so quickly and by so many different people, and partly because no one in authority, so far as we know, was imposing a particular text-type upon the churches. With the rise of monarchical bishops, the time arrived, in A.D. 382, when a Damasus was strong enough to be able to prescribe a certain text; and he did, in his case a Latin version. Such action tends to freeze text-types.

Alfred Martin, in his article in *Which Bible?*, does not really consider these facts when he protests: "Is it possible to believe that a text actually fabricated in the fourth century rapidly became so dominant that practically no copies were made any longer of exemplars which contained the type of text found in B and Aleph, also of the fourth century? That is really asking too much."[8]

---

8. "A Critical Examination of the Westcott-Hort Textual Theory," in *Which Bible?*, ed. David Otis Fuller, pp. 144–73.

In fact it is not asking too much, and it is just what the evidence argues for. The rise of the Byzantine tradition coincided with two things: the abandonment of Greek in places other than the eastern end of the empire, and the freezing of text-types.

Fee has recently advanced other reasons why the Byzantine text (which he loosely refers to as the TR) became dominant.[9] These include the following: (1) The influence of John Chrysostom can scarcely be overestimated. He used the Byzantine text in Antioch and carried it with him to Constantinople. By far the most popular preacher of the age, he exercised vast influence in popularizing that text throughout what was left of the Greek-speaking world.[10] (2) As the church became more and more institutionalized, manuscripts were copied and kept in monasteries, schools, and churches. This meant less interweaving of the textual traditions, more freezing, and more imposed unanimity in a given area.

Once the Byzantine tradition had been established for a few centuries in Constantinople and its empire, it would not be surprising to find many copies of this text-type. Moreover it would then be extremely difficult to argue at any point for a shorter text, because for the uninformed it would sound too much like removing words from God's revelation, even if in fact the text-type had added words to God's revelation.

Thesis 3: *The Byzantine text-type is demonstrably a secondary text.* I am not here arguing for or against a theory that sees the genesis of the Byzantine text as a systematic conflation of other texts, even though some conflation certainly occurred.

---

9. "Modern Textual Criticism and the Revival of the *Textus Receptus*," *JETS* 21 (1978): 19–33. This paper was originally delivered on 28 December 1976 at Westminster Theological Seminary, Philadelphia, at the 28th annual meeting of the Evangelical Theological Society. See also Zane C. Hodges, "Modern Textual Criticism and the Majority Text: A Response," *JETS* 21 (1978): 143–55; Fee, "Modern Textual Criticism and the Majority Text: A Rejoinder," *JETS* 21 (1978): 157–60; and Hodges, "Modern Textual Criticism and the Majority Text: A Surrejoinder," *JETS* 21 (1978): 161–64.

10. For a similar assessment of the spectacular influence of Chrysostom, cf. Edwin Charles Dargan, *A History of Preaching*, 2 vols. (1905–1912; reprint ed., Grand Rapids: Baker, 1954), 1:86–93. The significance of Chrysostom for textual criticism is further discussed in the appendix.

Rather, I am saying that textual critics who pore over manuscripts (or photographs and transcriptions of them) begin to detect clear signs of secondary influence. For example, harmonization is, indisputably, a secondary process. In general, scribes do not purposely introduce difficulties into the text; they try to resolve them. One might argue that particularly heterodox scribes might well make a text more complicated. However, a heterodox scribe is likely to change the theological content rather than relatively minor historical and geographical details; and in any case the Byzantine tradition does not reflect merely an odd manuscript given to harmonization, but rather the whole tradition. This is especially so in the Synoptic Gospels. In the article to which I have just referred, Fee points out a particular section in which the Byzantine text contains some thirty-eight major harmonizations, as compared with one harmonization in the Alexandrian text.[11] Thus prompted, I made some checks myself in other passages and found similar proportions. The only way to circumvent the evidence is to deny that they are harmonizations, or to argue that harmonizations are not secondary; and I find it very difficult to conceive how either of these alternatives can be defended by the person who has spent much time poring over the primary data.

Thesis 4: *The Alexandrian text-type has better credentials than any other text-type now available.* Some of the literature put out by defenders of the TR gives the impression that

---

11. Van Bruggen does not deny that such features are secondary, but he tries to weaken the force of the argument by saying that non-Byzantine text-types also have secondary features and that in any case secondary features are difficult to detect in the absence of the original. Moreover he argues that if the editors of the Byzantine text were out to harmonize and fit Gospel passages together, they missed most of their opportunities. *The Ancient Text of the New Testament,* pp. 30ff. However: (1) This last contention overlooks the fundamental distinction between intentional and unintentional errors; and even errors of the intentional type may not reflect the intention to achieve an overall smoothness. No one argues that the editors of the Byzantine text were self-consciously *trying* to produce such a consistent synthesis. (2) Although *some* secondary features are difficult to detect in the absence of the original, this does not apply equally to all, a point tacitly recognized by van Bruggen himself when he discovers secondary features in the non-Byzantine texts. (3) No one denies that non-Byzantine texts, as well as the Byzantine, give evidence of secondary influence; but the obvious point is that the Byzantine boasts *far more* secondary features than the others.

the great fourth-century uncials, Vaticanus (B) and Sinaiticus (א), are the only exemplars of the Alexandrian text; and therefore, it is argued, the Alexandrian text is itself a product of the fourth century.[12]

This is manifestly untrue, as the more able defenders of the TR have been forced to admit. Not only is the Alexandrian text-type found in some biblical quotations by ante-Nicene fathers, but the text-type is also attested by some of the early version witnesses. More convincing yet, Greek papyri from the second and third centuries have shown up, none of which reflects a Byzantine text and most of which have a mixed Alexandrian/Western text. The famous papyrus p[75], which dates from about A.D. 200 and is perhaps earlier, is astonishingly close to Vaticanus.[13] This find definitely proves the early date of the Vaticanus text-type.[14]

In addition it has been shown that the Alexandrian text has another point in its favor. Any text-type is either recensional or not recensional. By "recensional" I mean that a text has come into being by conscious revision, editing, or conflation, or by change over a period of time as part of a *directed* developing process. If this does not explain the genesis of a particular text, then that text is simply the copy of a copy of a copy: it is not a recension at all. If the latter were so in the case of B, it would mean that the Alexandrian tradition, especially as preserved in B and a few others, is the best text-type now extant: that is, it is closest to the original. And that is precisely

12. E.g., Jasper James Ray, *God Wrote Only One Bible* (Junction City, Oreg.: Eye Opener, 1970).

13. This has been clearly demonstrated and much discussed. For more recent bibliography cf. Everett F. Harrison, *Introduction to the New Testament,* rev. ed. (Grand Rapids: Eerdmans, 1971), p. 78; and articles by Gordon D. Fee.

14. This also overturns the so-called "Hesychian hypothesis." Hesychius, according to Jerome, produced an important revision of the Septuagint about A.D. 300, and some continental scholars have argued that Vaticanus came from the same hand. However, the existence of p[75] proves the text-type of Vaticanus antedates Hesychius by a century or more. By the same token, defenders of the Byzantine text who ascribe the development of the Alexandrian text to Origen (ca. 185–ca. 254) are ignoring this hard evidence.

the position being advanced in some recent first-class textual work.[15]

This does not mean that the Alexandrian tradition is to be preferred in all cases. The external evidence must be weighed text-type by text-type, and that evidence must in turn be weighed against the internal evidence. Even Westcott and Hort, after all, thought Byzantine readings were best in some instances. The consciousness that complexities exist is precisely what prompts the vast majority of contemporary textual critics, evangelical and otherwise, to opt for an eclectic text.

Thesis 5: *The argument to the effect that what the majority of believers in the history of the church have believed is true, is ambiguous at best and theologically dangerous at worst; and as applied to textual criticism, the argument proves nothing very helpful anyway.*

What do the terms "believers" and "church" here mean? Do we place the terms in the evangelical tradition and mean regenerate believers and "believers' church"? Might not this exclude Erasmus himself, the man behind the TR? Or by "believers" do we mean "adherents to the Christian faith," "Christian faith" being loosely defined and related vaguely to Christendom? How many believers in either case have ever thought through the problems of textual criticism and "believed" anything about the textual tradition? Most have just used what others around them have used.

Moreover such an argument, I suspect, would justify infant baptism, Arminianism (if not semi-Pelagianism!), and

---

15. Cf. Gordon D. Fee, "P75, P66, and Origen: The Myth of Early Textual Recension in Alexandria," in *New Dimensions in New Testament Study*, ed. Richard N. Longenecker and Merrill C. Tenney (Grand Rapids: Zondervan, 1974), pp. 19–45. Van Bruggen, ignoring these things, offers in *The Ancient Text of the New Testament* an argument that is really a classic non sequitur. He points out that the most-ancient witnesses do not represent a uniform text-type and that contemporary textual critics offer diverse eclectic texts, and from these true observations he argues that it is better to follow the Byzantine text. I cannot see why this should be so. Textual critics now have an abundance of evidence from which it is frequently difficult to decide which text-type is superior: why should it be thought better to return to any one text-type exclusively when God in His providence has provided us with such wealth?

other viewpoints to which at least some Christian readers would not likely give assent. Since when has majority opinion defined what is true, even majority evangelical opinion? Logically speaking, a proposition is either true (that is, it accords with reality and is held to be true by omniscience), or it is not, even if not one person believes it. Of course one should be very careful and humble before disagreeing dogmatically with what the majority of believers (whoever they are) have held to be true; but the fact that they believe it does not make it true, nor does it entail the falsity of any counterbelief.

Even if we were to accept such an argument, however, I doubt that it would confirm the rightness of adopting the Byzantine text-type. From the fourth century to the Reformation, "believers" (however defined) in the West used the Latin Vulgate: would not that historical fact in 1450 mean that it was wrong to appeal to the Greek text instead of to the established Latin version?[16]

Thesis 6: *The argument that defends the Byzantine text by appealing to the providence of God is logically and theologically fallacious.*

This argument is akin to that discussed under thesis 5. I am suspicious of propositional arguments that rest too much on providence, because divine providence can be variously interpreted.[17] This is not to deny the providence of God: far from it. But it is to deny that everything that takes place under divine providence is morally good or necessarily true. To say this does not ascribe evil to God. Divine sovereignty is so all-embracing that it stands behind all things, including both John Calvin and Adolf Hitler. Such divine sovereignty is, however, asymmetrical: it stands behind Calvin and Hitler in different ways, such that the good produced is always traceable, in the

---

16. Van Bruggen wants to rehabilitate the Byzantine text because, among other things, it is the text that "the churches of the great Reformation deliberately adopted." *The Ancient Text of the New Testament,* p. 36. Unfortunately he does not mention that they had no other option available to them!

17. A fascinating example is Oliver Cromwell, who based many decisions on his reading of providence. Cf. Antonia Fraser, *Cromwell: The Lord Protector* (New York: Knopf, 1973).

last analysis, to God, while the evil produced is not traceable to Him in the same way.

God, it is argued, has providentially preserved the Byzantine tradition. That is true; but He has also providentially preserved the Western, Caesarean, and Alexandrian traditions. Yet has not God preserved the Byzantine text-type for at least a millennium, during which time the others were unknown? True enough; but He preserved it in one small corner of the world, apart from which the Latin Vulgate reigned preeminent, a version based primarily on a Western textual tradition.

What too of the great men of God who relied on non-Byzantine texts, such as those of the first three centuries, or men like Benjamin B. Warfield, J. Gresham Machen, A. T. Robertson, James I. Packer, and many more: did God's providence fail in their case? The Westminster Confession of Faith, and its counterpart, the Baptist Confession of 1689, are quite correct to attest to God's "singular care and providence" inasmuch as the text has been "kept pure in *all ages* (1.8, italics mine); but "all ages" surely includes the first, second, and third centuries, not to mention the nineteenth and twentieth. Because this is so, we cannot understand "kept pure" to mean that each manuscript agrees perfectly with the other, since no manuscript agrees perfectly with any other. What is at stake is a purity of text of such a substantial nature that nothing we believe to be doctrinally true, and nothing we are commanded to do, is in any way jeopardized by the variants. This is true for *any* textual tradition. The interpretation of individual passages may well be called in question; but never is a doctrine affected.[18]

World population is growing rapidly. A large and growing number of Christians speak and read in languages other than English, and most of these people, if they have a translation, have one that is not based exclusively on the Byzantine text. Moreover a growing number of English-speaking people are using versions other than the KJV, and none of these versions is based exclusively on the Byzantine textual tradition. It

18. This point will receive greater treatment in thesis 9.

would not surprise me if a majority of "believers" in the world today read such versions. If the majority has not yet been reached, I imagine it will be in a few years. And because of the combination of population growth-rates and the rise in world literacy, only a few more years would have to elapse before more people would be reading versions based on non-Byzantine texts than have *ever* read Byzantine-based versions. Will those who appeal to the argument from providence then concede that divine providence is justifying this development? If they do not and instead write the development off as apostasy, they are guilty of gross inconsistency, and so the argument cannot be trusted. If they do concede it, then their present defense of the Byzantine text will have been shown to be erroneous, and so again one will have to conclude that something is wrong with the argument.

Thesis 7: *The argument that appeals to fourth-century writing practices to deny the possibility that the Byzantine text is a conflation, is fallacious.* Hills, in his book *The King James Version Defended!* argues that the Byzantine text could not be a fourth-century compilation from other texts because editors of that period did not have desks to write on.[19] He is mistaken in both premise and conclusion. Although many fourth-century writers used no desks, and none sat at a desk as we do today, nevertheless some stood at desks to write.[20] In any case, in A.D. 170 Tatian wrote his *Diatessaron*, essentially a harmony of the four canonical Gospels; so obviously he managed to have several manuscripts around him. Moreover if the Byzantine text is a conflation, it may well be a conflation that developed in several stages. In that case not all contributory manuscripts needed to be present at one time. This seventh thesis deserves mention only because Hills's argument has been repeated in some of the more popular literature.

Thesis 8: *Textual arguments that depend on adopting the TR and comparing other text-types with it are guilty, me-*

19. *The King James Version Defended! A Space-Age Defense of the Historic Christian Faith* (Des Moines: Christian Research, 1973), p. 177.

20. Cf. Metzger, *The Text of the New Testament*, pp. 16–18, and the literature there cited.

thodologically speaking, of begging the issue; and in any case they present less than the whole truth.

I have in front of me, as I write this, a little pamphlet called "New Eye Opener," by Jasper James Ray. The subtitle is: "200 key references show how all modern Bibles differ from the King James Version, and the Greek Textus Receptus from which it was translated." This tract is simply one example of a kind of argument frequently found in the writings of the defenders of the TR and KJV. It begins by presupposing that the TR, and therefore the KJV, constitute the final and irrefutable form of God's Word. Then by comparing other English versions that change this or that, or leave out the other, it castigates them for their omissions and changes.

Methodologically this kind of argument is quite unacceptable, for it assumes what is in fact to be proved. Because many people have a deep personal attachment to the KJV forged by many years of intimate use, they will by this argument as often as not feel reinforced in their commitment to the KJV. But supposing the TR is not as close to the original as, for example, the Alexandrian text-type, what then? What Ray's tract *actually* proves is that most modern versions differ from the KJV in the places that he carefully selects. If I began with, say, the *New International Version* (NIV), I could show all the places where the KJV disagreed with it. But such arguments do not themselves demonstrate the authenticity of the rendering of any version at any particular place. Methodologically speaking, they beg the issue.

The problem is even deeper than that. Although it is true that most modern translations omit words or phrases or (occasionally) verses which the KJV retains, nevertheless two observations will make it clear that less than the whole truth is being presented.

First, there are a few instances in which the KJV omits words or phrases that the other versions retain. For example, in I John 3:1 the KJV reads, "Behold, what manner of love the Father hath bestowed upon us, that we should be called the sons of God: therefore the world knoweth us not. . . ." The NIV, however, reads, "How great is the love the Father has lavished on us, that we should be called children of God! *And that*

is what we are! The reason the world does not know us. . . ."[21]
The KJV omits the Greek *kai esmen*. Again, in Jude 25 the KJV
has, "To the only wise God our Saviour, be glory and majesty,
dominion and power, both now and ever. Amen." The NIV
omits "wise" but adds two important phrases, including a reference to Jesus Christ: ". . . to the only God our Savior be
glory, majesty, power and authority, *through Jesus Christ our
Lord, before all ages,* now and forevermore! Amen." If I were
being vindictive, I would suggest that the translators of the
KJV were heretical modernists who were trying to expunge references to Jesus Christ as mediator. . . .

Second, not all of Ray's references are based on a clear-
cut difference between the Byzantine tradition and the other
text-types, even if he lumps them all together. For example, he
includes I John 5:7-8, the trinitarian formula I discussed earlier, as one of the passages that modern versions change or
omit. The words in question are found in the TR; but they are
certainly not an integral part of the Byzantine textual tradition. Some defenders of the KJV now admit that the *Comma
Johanneum* forms no part of the original text; but not a few
still cite the following somewhat-abbreviated paragraph from
John Gill's *Exposition of the New Testament:*

> As to its being wanting in some Greek manuscripts, as the
> Alexandrian and others, it need only be said that it is to be
> found in many others; it is in an old British copy, and in the
> Complutensian edition, the compilers of which made use of
> various copies; and out of sixteen ancient copies of Robert
> Stephens', nine of them had it: and as to its not being cited by
> some of the ancient Fathers, this can be no sufficient proof of
> the spuriousness of it, since it might be in the original copy,
> though not in the copies used by them, through the carelessness
> or unfaithfulness of transcribers; or it might be in their copies,
> and yet not cited by them, they having Scripture enough with-
> out it to defend the doctrine of the Trinity, and the divinity of
> Christ: and yet after all, certain it is, that it is cited by many of
> them; by Fulgentius in the beginning of the sixth century,
> against the Arians, without any scruple or hesitation; and
> Jerome, as had been observed before has it in his translation

21. Italics mine.

made in the latter part of the fourth century. In his epistle to Eustochium prefixed to his translation of the canonical epistles, he complains of the omission of it by unfaithful interpreters. It is cited by Athanasius about the year 350; and before him by Cyprian, in the middle of the third century, about the year 250; and is referred to by Tertullian about the year 200; and which was within a hundred years, or a little more, of the writing of the epistle; which may be enough to satisfy anyone of the genuineness of the passage; and besides there was never any dispute over it till Erasmus left it out of the first edition of his translation of the New Testament; and yet he himself upon the credit of the old British copy before mentioned, put it into another edition of his translation.[22]

So many remarks could be offered in response to this quotation that it is difficult to know where to begin. In addition to what I wrote on this question earlier in this volume, I offer these few points: (1) Gill lived from 1697 to 1771. Therefore he was unacquainted with the vast majority of the most ancient textual evidence, since most of it was still unknown in his day. (2) The *Comma Johanneum* is *not* found in "many other" Greek manuscripts, nor in nine of the sixteen used by Stephanus. It is found in precisely four Greek manuscripts, at least three of which (and probably all of which) postdate Erasmus's *second* edition. Gill is wrong about the facts. (3) The "ancient" copies of Stephanus did not antedate the tenth century! (4) The "old British copy" to which Gill refers is minuscule 61, the codex written *after* Erasmus's second edition, apparently in order to force Erasmus to include the *Comma* in his subsequent editions. (5) Although Erasmus did indeed put the *Comma* into the text after this "old British copy" was found, he protested in a lengthy footnote that he did so under duress and that he still judged the *Comma* to be non-original. Why does Gill not mention these facts? Or at least,

---

22. John Gill, *An Exposition of the New Testament,* 3 vols. (1746–1748; reprint ed., Atlanta: Turner Lassetter, 1954), 2:907–8. This paragraph has been cited in several publications, including a little booklet called *The Providential Preservation of the Greek Text of the New Testament* (see p. 25), which culls material from various defenders of the TR, and which is said to be compiled by "Ergatees." Van Bruggen, in *The Ancient Text of the New Testament,* is one of the few who defend the Byzantine text but not the TR.

why do not the modern defenders of the authenticity of the passages do so? (6) In some of the fathers cited by Gill, the words are not cited as Scripture, but, as I indicated earlier, probably arose as allegorical exegesis of the three witnesses. (7) The *Comma Johanneum* did not become established in the Old Latin until the fifth century. (8) It does *not* appear in Jerome's Vulgate, despite what Gill says. Gill makes the common mistake of thinking that the Vulgate used in his own day is exactly the same as it was when it left Jerome's hands. This is demonstrably untrue: the Vulgate underwent a whole series of revisions. The *Comma Johanneum* does not appear in the Vulgate until the beginning of the ninth century or thereabouts. (9) To say "there was never any dispute over it till Erasmus left it out of the first edition of his translation of the New Testament" is factually incorrect. First, Erasmus was not simply producing a *translation* of the New Testament (that is, a version), but a printed *Greek text* of the New Testament. Second, in the Eastern church, where Greek was still being used, *not one* Greek manuscript included the *Comma Johanneum*. Third, as I have already shown, before Erasmus's time the Vulgate had reigned supreme for several hundred years; few in the West knew Greek. The Vulgate by A.D. 800 or so included it; and that explains the adoption of the reading in the West. Fourth, the argument that what is long held as traditionally correct is God's truth is, methodologically speaking, the same as the one used to justify the worst features of the Roman Catholic tradition at the time of Martin Luther: the appeal to long-established tradition. (10) The Complutensian edition of which Gill speaks is slightly older than that of Erasmus. However, it included the *Comma Johanneum* because it found it in the Vulgate. As far as we know, it had *no* Greek manuscript evidence for the reading.

Let me emphatically deny that by endorsing the omission of the *Comma Johanneum* I am rejecting the doctrine of the Trinity or the deity of Christ. On the doctrinal question I shall say a little more in the next thesis. The point I am making at the moment is simpler, namely, that it is methodologically improper to begin with the TR or the KJV and judge all readings on the basis of this point of departure. Such a method cannot help but slant things in a predetermined direction; but slanted arguments in these issues ought to be rejected by lovers of truth (cf. thesis 13 below).

Thesis 9: *The charge that the non-Byzantine text-types are theologically aberrant is fallacious.*

A great deal of the heat with which this question is discussed is generated by the conviction of most defenders of the TR that non-Byzantine texts are theologically aberrant. Of course if their charge can be substantiated, that settles the issue. For example, no one today, to my knowledge, accepts the Marcionite canon: all agree Marcion and/or his followers tampered with the text of Scripture by removing major parts of it (whole chapters and books). However, I would argue that none of the text-types distinguished by contemporary textual criticism is theologically heretical in the way that defenders of the KJV sometimes suggest.

The first thing to remember is the number of ways errors can be introduced into manuscripts. The vast majority of manuscript errors are of the "unintentional" variety; and most of the "intentional" changes arise out of a desire to correct or improve the grammar, spelling, or logical cohesion. When an intentional change affects the meaning of the passage, there is a demonstrable tendency to move the meaning in the direction of the orthodoxy and forms of piety current at the time, not away from it. By "demonstrable" I mean that even *within* the Byzantine tradition, the later witnesses are inclined to change things in favor of giving *more* titles to Christ, not fewer; in favor of using *more* liturgical phrases and explanatory asides, not fewer.

The second thing to note is the fact that the omission of an individual title or phrase or verse does not constitute evidence for theological heresy. Perhaps the omission was part of the original, and the manuscripts that include the title or phrase or verse are guilty of additions. Beyond that, however, even if the omission were not part of the autograph, the omission per se would not prove heterodoxy. One would have to ask *why* the omission had taken place. The reason might prove to be nothing more than homoeoteleuton.[23] Moreover, before arguing that an individual manuscript or text-type is at some particular reference interested in denying a specific doctrine, it would be necessary to show that the manuscript or text-type in question consistently tries to suppress or deny that doctrine.

What we discover in practice is that most changes or omissions (or additions, depending on the point of view) are "quite trivial and wholly devoid of theological significance."[24] Where they do affect the meaning of a passage in such a way that the passage can no longer be called upon to support a particular doctrine, nevertheless the doctrine itself remains unchanged because it is still supported by many other passages found in the same textual tradition. One must conclude, therefore, that if a heretic changed the particular passage in order to suppress some specific doctrine, then he was singularly incompetent if he did not systematically change all the other places in the document that supported the same doctrine.

I suppose that no doctrine is more repeatedly thought to be under attack in the non-Byzantine traditions, according to the defenders of the KJV, than the doctrine of the deity of Christ. Yet what I have said applies to this doctrine as comprehensively as to any other. To prove it in detail would presuppose in the reader a fair degree of competence in Greek, so I shall pass up the opportunity. Instead I shall demonstrate the general point by an analogous argument. In a recent article Victor Perry discusses the places in the New Testament where the Greek *can* be understood (either by the right choice of witnesses or by the appropriate grammatical interpretation) to call Jesus "God," quite specifically.[25] In his chart, a simplified form of which I here reproduce in chart 1, he provides a neat summary of the places in the New Testament where various

---

23. For example, because the last five words of Luke 14:26 and 14:27 are exactly the same in Greek, it is easy to understand the omission of the latter verse in about a dozen manuscripts.

24. Donald MacLeod, "The Bible and Textual Criticism," *BanT*, no. 111 (1972): 12–26. This excellent essay says in brief compass what I here detail at greater length.

25. "Problem Passages of the New Testament in Some Modern Translations: Does the New Testament Call Jesus God?" *ET* 87 (1975–76): 214–15.

versions call Jesus "God." A check (✓) means the version in question does directly ascribe deity to Jesus; a cross (X) means it does not. Most of the abbreviations listed are well known; any questions, however, may be referred to the list of abbreviations on page 8. *Mg.* means "marginal reading."

CHART 1

	John 1:1	John 1:18	Acts 20:28	Rom. 9:5	II Thess. 1:12	Titus 2:13	Heb. 1:8	II Peter 1:1
KJV	✓	X	✓	✓	X	X	✓	X
RV	✓	X	✓	✓	X	✓	✓	✓
RV mg.		✓	X	X		X		X
RSV	✓	X	X	X	X	✓	✓	✓
RSV mg.		✓	X	✓		X	X	X
NEB	✓	X	X	X	X	✓	✓	✓
NEB mg.		✓	X	✓		X	X	
Moffatt	X	X	X	X	X	X	X	✓
Goodspeed	X	X	✓	X	X	✓	X	✓
TEV	✓	✓	X	X	X	✓	✓	✓
TEV mg.		X	X	✓				
NIV	✓	✓	✓	✓	X	✓	✓	✓
NIV mg.		X	X	X	✓			
MLB	✓	X	✓	✓	X	✓	✓	✓
NWT	X	X	X	X	X	X	X	X

A number of observations may draw attention to the most important results: (1) Only the NWT omits all specific references to Jesus' deity; and that of course is predictable. (2) Even James Moffatt and Edgar J. Goodspeed, whose liberal propensities are well-known, manage one and three references, respectively. (3) The KJV accepts only four of the eight as references to Jesus' deity. (4) The highest number of such references belongs to the NIV, a translation done by evangelicals but based on an eclectic text.

Of course the doctrine of Jesus' deity does not depend exclusively on the passages that explicitly call Him "God"; but the point I am making is that the doctrine of the deity of Jesus Christ is affirmed by all of the above translations, with the understandable exception of NWT. By this I am far from suggesting that each of these translations is of equal value. I am simply pointing out that individual passages may be interpreted variously, or different textual traditions for such passages may prompt two or three mutually exclusive meanings, without the denial of an entire doctrine.

But, someone objects, suppose a particular doctrine is based on just one verse: would that not place the doctrine in jeopardy, subject to the whim of textual criticism? Yes, I suppose it would. This never happens, however, for the simple reason that established doctrines are never based on just one verse. Few are likely to formulate a doctrine that depends on only one passage. "What!" someone replies, "How many times does the Bible have to say something for it to be true?" The answer of course is that the Bible does not have to say it at all for it to be true. Either it is true or it is not. But the Bible may have to say it several different times, and perhaps in different ways, for us to understand unambiguously and precisely what truth is being taught. And that is precisely why doctrine is not based on just one verse.

In brief I am arguing that all the textual traditions are orthodox, not least in the sense that all of them teach the doctrines that the defenders of the KJV construe as the ingredients of orthodoxy. *Some* modern translations tend toward the heretical by virtue of the force of the presuppositions that govern the *translation;* but the texts underlying those translations are a different matter.

This ninth thesis is defensible even in the case of a long omission, such as the omission of the long ending of Mark. In fact almost all of the material in the long ending (Mark 16:9-20 KJV) is found in Luke. The most remarkable exception is Mark 16:18a ("They shall take up serpents; and if they drink any deadly thing, it shall not hurt them"). And even this finds corroboration in Acts 28:3-6. I am not here arguing for or against the authenticity of Mark 16:9-20. The textual evidence is extremely complex.[26] My point is simply that one

26. Besides John W. Burgon, *The Last Twelve Verses of the Gospel According to S. Mark,* a more recent volume has ventured support for the long

of the shorter texts is not demonstrably theologically aberrant, and no text-type can be dismissed in toto on theological grounds.

This ninth thesis finds unwitting support in the writings of Jasper James Ray, one of the most polemical of the defenders of the TR. In his book, *God Wrote Only One Bible*, he invites his readers to examine "all the rest of the 5,337 changes made in the Textus Receptus by Westcott's and Hort's Greek Text," promising that they will always discover that the additional passages found in the longer text (the TR) are never "in any whit contrary to God's revelation."[27] That he can affirm this suggests, *mutatis mutandis,* that God's revelation is sufficiently intact without these additions that it can provide a norm for judging them. It is difficult then to see why the shorter texts are judged heretical. Therefore the charge that the non-Byzantine text-types are theologically aberrant is fallacious.

It follows that the language of most of the TR's defenders needs to be greatly moderated. On this I shall have more to say.

Thesis 10: *The KJV was not accepted without a struggle, and some outstanding believers soon wanted to replace it.* This is simply a historical fact. The Great Bible continued to be published until 1644, thirty-three years after the KJV first appeared. One reason for the eventual acceptance of the KJV was its excellence, despite the fact that Hugh Broughton declared that he "had rather be rent in pieces by wild horses, than any such translation by my consent should be urged upon poor churches";[28] but another reason lay in the fact that the KJV was appointed to be read in the Church of England, an ecclesiastical body sufficiently hierarchical that formal uniformity could be made to prevail, and so influential as to touch all

---

ending: William R. Farmer, *The Last Twelve Verses of Mark* (New York: Cambridge University, 1974). Most New Testament scholars, both conservative and otherwise, have not been convinced by Farmer's arguments; but he presents as good a case as can be made.

27. Pp. 105–6.

28. Cited by F. F. Bruce, *The Books and the Parchments: Some Chapters on the Transmission of the Bible,* 3d ed. (Westwood, N.J.: Revell, 1963), p. 229.

others in that restricted, English-speaking world. Although the KJV received no more "authorization" than this, it rapidly took root, especially during the ensuing decades when Puritan influence crested and made the Bible an integral part of English life.

It is also a fact of history that several voices were raised at an early period, promoting the revision of the KJV. Brian Walton (ca. 1600-1661), editor of the famous *Biblia Sacra Polyglotta*[29] and, considering the materials he had available, no mean textual scholar, was one of these; and he did so on textual grounds. Of course someone might object that because Walton did not stand in the Puritan tradition, he was trying to tamper with the text. Anyone who has worked hard at Walton's magnum opus must dismiss the charge as preposterous.[30] Moreover in 1660 a number of Presbyterian and Puritan ministers presented to the bishops an "Exception Against the Book of Common Prayer," whose eighth point reads: "A new Royal translation of the Scriptures is to be uniformly introduced."[31] This demonstrates that the pressure to revise the KJV sprang from diverse circles.

I make these points not because they prove the imperfection of the KJV, but because they inject a little historical perspective into the question at hand.

Thesis 11: *The Byzantine text-type must not be thought to be the precise equivalent of the TR.* This important point is too often ignored. The TR is based on a mere handful of relatively late manuscripts, in comparison with the thousands of

---

29. 6 vols. (London: Thomas Roycroft, 1653-1657). This was among the first works in England to have been published by subscription. Nine languages are represented, although usually no more than eight appear at a time. Moreover, in addition to printing, for example, the Hebrew, LXX, Syriac, and Aramaic of some Old Testament passages, Walton included his own Latin translation of the original and of each version.

30. While studying at Cambridge University, I spent a great deal of time in this magisterial work and came away quite awed. Despite the advances made in many areas since its publication, in some ways Walton's work "has not yet been superseded" (ODC, p. 1458).

31. Cf. Horton Davis, *The Worship of the English Puritans* (Westminster: Dacre, 1948), pp. 14ff. For this reference I am indebted to my good friend and stimulating colleague, Rev. Roy Williams.

witnesses that attest the Byzantine tradition. It is true of course that the TR is based on manuscripts of that tradition and stands fairly close to the broader tradition of which it forms a part; but the fact remains that it does not consider the broad evidence of its own tradition. It is also a fact that the closest manuscripts within a textual tradition average about six to ten variants per chapter. The importance of these observations becomes clear in the next thesis.

Thesis 12: *The argument that ties the adoption of the TR to verbal inspiration is logically and theologically fallacious.*

The confusion against which this twelfth thesis contends is becoming so common that it ought to evoke real alarm, because it reflects two serious misapprehensions. The first concerns the nature and purpose of textual criticism; the second concerns the nature and definition of verbal inspiration.

That the two questions are intimately related in the minds of the defenders of the TR is abundantly clear from the most casual perusal of their literature. In support of their argument they cite both the well-known passages that affirm the inspiration of Scripture and a few less-common ones that affirm the sanctity and immutability of God's *words*. I quote a few examples (all from the KJV):

"Ye shall not add unto the word which I command you, neither shall ye diminish ought from it, that ye may keep the commandments of the Lord your God which I command you." (Deut. 4:2)

"Every word of God is pure: he is a shield unto them that put their trust in him. Add thou not unto his words, lest he reprove thee, and thou be found a liar." (Prov. 30:5-6)

"And if any man shall take away from the words of the book of this prophecy, God shall take away his part out of the book of life, and out of the holy city, and from the things which are written in this book." (Rev. 22:19)

"For ever, O Lord, thy word is settled in heaven." (Ps. 119:89)[32]

These passages and a few others are constantly called forth to justify the adoption of the TR. Indeed they are fre-

---

32. E.g., Ray, *God Wrote Only One Bible*, pp. 120-21.

quently cited as if their existence *entails* the adoption of the TR. The argument, briefly, is this: Since God inspired the Scriptures verbally, therefore He must have preserved them even to the details of their words; and these passages presuppose that God has done just that. Based on arguments that I have already refuted, such as the fact that the Byzantine tradition takes in the majority of the manuscripts or that it has been providentially preserved, the TR is claimed by its defenders to be the text that God has specially anointed. Suspicion that this is not so is then transformed in their eyes into suspicion that the doctrine of verbal inspiration is being denied.

I shall reply by making four points.

First, even if their interpretation of the biblical passages just cited were correct, they would be left with an insoluble problem in the Byzantine tradition itself. I pointed out in thesis 11 that no two manuscripts in the Byzantine tradition agree perfectly. If, however, their theological argument is to be taken in the rigorous way they seem to want to take it, their own preferred text-type falls under condemnation along with the other text-types. There is only a difference of degree between the textual variants that exist within one textual tradition and the textual variants found when two or more textual traditions are compared. If verbal inspiration is theologically tied to one textual tradition, it does not escape the kind of problems presented if more than one textual tradition be admitted.

I would argue, moreover, that the TR in particular has major problems to overcome. It remains a fact that a dozen or so readings in the KJV find no support in any Greek manuscript whatsoever. In the last few verses of Revelation, a half dozen such inventions occur. These can be traced directly to the fact that Erasmus had to prepare a Greek manuscript for these verses by translating back from the Vulgate.[33] Now if the verses cited by the defenders of the KJV condemn those who *omit* or *change* God's words, they equally condemn those who *add* to God's words. To be consistent, these defenders must urge us to throw away our KJV Bibles along with the other

33. I have discussed this point already: cf. p. 34 above.

"perversions" of which they are prone to speak. This, then, is the first logical difficulty with their argument.

There is a second logical point to be observed. Even if the biblical passages they cite entail some such conclusion as the idea that one or another of the textual traditions must be pre-eminently pure, it would not necessarily follow that the text in question is the Byzantine.

Thus, when I turn to John 5:3b–4 and discover it is missing from the earliest witnesses, which constitute a wide geographical distribution indeed, I conclude it was not in the original. And, as I shall show, I am not denying the doctrine of verbal inspiration by such a conclusion; which brings me to the next point.

Second, it is extremely important to understand what is meant, and what is not meant, by saying that the Bible "as originally written . . . is verbally and plenarily inspired."[34] "Plenarily" means "fully." "Verbally" means that the inspiration extends even to the words written. In passing, I should point out that "verbally" does *not* entail the conclusion that the Bible was *dictated* by God. Most of it, according to its own witness, was not given in so immediate a fashion. Hence it is possible to distinguish between the writing style of, say, Paul, and that of John. However, the inclusion of the word "verbally" is designed to protect us from vague notions of inspiration that suggest the human authors "felt inspired" or were "inspired" as to the general drift but not in the detail, or that their writings witness to the inspiration of their authors. In fact, divine inspiration so operated that even where the human authors were hammering out their own deeply felt and very personal concerns (for example, II Cor. 10–13), the result was *theopneustos,* God-breathed (II Tim. 3:16), even to the detail of the words used.[35]

---

34. Article 1 of the Articles of Faith to which Northwest Baptist Theological College and Seminary adhere.

35. Among the best books on the subject are: Benjamin B. Warfield, *The Inspiration and Authority of the Bible,* ed. Samuel G. Craig (Philadelphia: Presbyterian and Reformed, 1948); Carl F. H. Henry, ed., *Revelation and the Bible: Contemporary Evangelical Thought* (1958; reprint ed., Grand Rapids: Baker, 1959); James I. Packer, *"Fundamentalism" and the Word of*

Another way of saying this without using the word *verbally* (although I have no objection to the term provided its meaning and purpose be rightly observed) is found in the now-famous "Ligonier Statement," signed by John M. Frame, John H. Gerstner, Peter R. Jones, John Warwick Montgomery, James I. Packer, Clark H. Pinnock, and Robert C. Sproul:

> We believe the Holy Scriptures of the Old and New Testaments to be the inspired and inerrant Word of God: We hold the Bible, as originally given through human agents of revelation, to be infallible and see this as a crucial article of faith with implications for the entire life and practice of all Christian people. With the great fathers of Christian history we declare our confidence in the total trustworthiness of the Scriptures, urging that any view which imputes to them a lesser degree of inerrancy than total, is in conflict with the Bible's self-testimony in general and with the teaching of Jesus Christ in particular. Out of obedience to the Lord of the Church we submit ourselves unreservedly to his authoritative view of Holy Writ.[36]

As far as I know, none of the subscribers to this statement accepts the preeminence of the Byzantine text. In fact, I cannot think of a single great theological writer who has given his energies to defend a high view of Scripture and who has adopted the TR, since the discovery of the great uncials and, later, the papyri and other finds. The theologically and biblically sensitive and precise writings of such men as Benjamin B. Warfield, James I. Packer, John W. Wenham, and others all defend "inspiration" in the classic sense, but none of them feels forced to follow the TR as a result.

In fact, besides the defenders of the TR, the people most likely to tie in "inspiration" with textual criticism are those just *outside* the evangelical camp. For example, Vincent Taylor observes that no two manuscripts of the New Testament agree,

---

God: Some Evangelical Principles (Grand Rapids: Eerdmans, 1958); John W. Wenham, *Christ and the Bible* (Downers Grove, Ill.: InterVarsity, 1973); and John Warwick Montgomery, ed., *God's Inerrant Word: An International Symposium on the Trustworthiness of Scripture* (Minneapolis: Bethany Fellowship, 1974). There are others, of course; but I doubt if there are better ones available.

36. Published in *God's Inerrant Word*, ed. John Warwick Montgomery, p. 7.

and he concludes: "This fact alone suggests that, while the Scriptures are inspired, they are not verbally inspired: otherwise it is difficult to think that so great a disparity would exist."[37] Now Taylor was a fine scholar, but his generally high caliber sags a little here. I know of no one who claims any one particular extant manuscript is inerrant. And to claim a particular text-type is inerrant is meaningless because a text-type is established by comparing manuscripts, grouping those with most features in common, and accepting the most probable readings. Therefore whenever verbal inspiration has been affirmed or presupposed, it has been ascribed only to the autographs.

Now both of the above statements, the Ligonier Statement and the shorter one I offered before it, stress the fact that inerrancy, infallibility, or any other similar term or phrase, obtains in the original documents, the autographs. It is a simple fact that we do not possess these autographs. Does this mean we are lost in a sea of uncertainty? Does it mean we possess nothing but a relatively inspired Bible after all?

These questions bring me to the third point, which I shall take up in a moment; but first of all I must return to the biblical passages cited at the beginning of this thesis. Not one of them promises an infallible text-type. Curses are laid on those who tamper with the text; and that ought to prompt copyists to work with care. Nevertheless I suspect the curse also pertains to the addition of nonrevelatory material to the corpus of biblical truth, as if it were equally inspired; or to the subtraction of biblical content from our lives, our churches, our homes, our creeds, whether willfully or by virtue of ignoring that part. How many of us who call ourselves "evangelicals" are so locked in to our own traditions, with their forms and their "do's and don't's," that we can scarcely distinguish such secondary material from the uniquely binding authority of Scripture? How many of us ignore major doctrines, or do not trouble ourselves to attain a thorough grasp of the basic content of

37. *The Text of the New Testament: A Short Introduction,* 2d ed. (London: Macmillan, 1963), p. 2.

each book of the Bible? With such questions as these do such biblical passages concern themselves. Moreover they attest to the *verbal* inspiration of Scripture in the sense discussed above. But they do not entail the adoption of a particular textual tradition.

Hence, if the first point demonstrates the logical fallacy of tying verbal inspiration to the Byzantine text, this second point outlines the theological fallacy.

Third, to concede that total inerrancy or verbal inspiration is restricted to the autographs does not mean we have no sure word from God. This point is well discussed by Montgomery.[38] I shall not repeat all his arguments here, as his work is readily available. I shall merely offer a condensation of some of his more important points, all of which he discusses more ably than I, and add one or two of my own remarks.

(1) A large conceptual distance exists between the statement, "The Scriptures as originally given are not inerrant," and the statement, "The Scriptures as originally given are inerrant, even if we do not have the autographs." (2) Textual criticism enables us to say, "William Shakespeare wrote, 'To be or not to be,' " even if we have no autograph to prove it. In like fashion the vast majority of the New Testament is textually certain. (3) Even where the text is less than certain, high probability of this reading or that exists. (4) No doctrine and no ethical command is affected by the "probability" passages, but only the precise meaning of specific passages. (5) In my judgment the degree of uncertainty raised by textual questions is a great deal less than the degree of uncertainty raised by hermeneutical questions. In other words, even when the text is certain there is often an honest difference of opinion among interpreters as to the precise meaning of the passage. Few evangelicals, I would like to think, will claim infallibility for their interpretations of the Scriptures; they are prepared to live with the (relatively) small degree of uncertainty raised by such limitations. The doubt raised by *textual* uncertainties, I submit, is far, far smaller. (6) As Montgomery points out, as we go

38. Montgomery, "Biblical Inerrancy: What Is at Stake?," in *God's Inerrant Word,* ed. John Warwick Montgomery, pp. 35ff.

back along the manuscript traditions the demonstrable errors thin out. Therefore it is reasonable to believe that if we could close the gap between our textual traditions and the autographs, all errors would be eliminated.[39] (7) On the epistemological question—a subject too vast to be adequately probed in this paper—I agree that the "evidence for biblical inerrancy . . . is never *itself* inerrant, but this by no means makes the inerrancy claim irrational."[40]

Fourth, the purpose and goal of textual criticism is to get as close to the original text as possible. To fail to recognize this is to misapprehend what textual criticism is all about.[41]

Thesis 13: *Arguments that attempt to draw textual conclusions from a prejudicial selection of not immediately relevant data, or from a slanted use of terms, or by a slurring appeal to guilt by association, or by repeated appeal to false evidence, are not only misleading, but ought to be categorically rejected by Christians who, above all others, profess both to love truth and to love their brothers in Christ.*

The practices against which this thesis contends are so common that detailed documentation would immediately double the length of this book. I offer but a few examples.

One brief pamphlet before me condemns the 1881 revisers as Romanists because some of their readings are akin to the Roman Catholic Vulgate. Why does it not point out that Erasmus, unlike Luther and Calvin, never left the Roman Catholic church? Besides, if the argument of this pamphlet were rigorously applied, I suppose I would have to give up singing hymns written by the famous nineteenth-century writer F. W. Faber (1814–1863), who followed John Henry Newman into the Roman Catholic church; and I confess to a cer-

---

39. This is not a good argument for inerrancy per se, against the doubt of the person who denies inerrancy; for surely all that could be concluded by the evidence is that all copies came from one manuscript, not that that manuscript was necessarily inerrant. However, the argument as I have presented it does forcefully show that the proliferation of variants is no substantive evidence *against* the inerrancy of autographs.

40. Montgomery, "Biblical Inerrancy: What Is at Stake?," p. 38.

41. For a recent article on the present status of textual criticism, cf. Eldon Jay Epp, "The Twentieth Century Interlude in New Testament Textual Criticism," *JBL* 93 (1974): 386–414.

tain reluctance in abandoning hymns like "My God, how wonderful Thou art," "Souls of men, why will ye scatter," "There's a wideness in God's mercy," and "Faith of our fathers."

Another little book in front of me slates such expressions as "intrinsic probability" and "transcriptional probability." The author thinks they belong to methods that are "not according to sound rules of Bible interpretation."[42] He asks, "Do you want to trust your soul to a probability?" No, of course I do not. I prefer to trust my soul to Christ. However, I should point out that deciding which manuscripts *within the Byzantine tradition* are to be followed at any variant reading involves questions of transcriptional probability.

Westcott and Hort are regularly portrayed in nearly diabolical garb; and Origen fares even worse, as the genesis of the non-Byzantine texts is regularly ascribed to him. The fact remains that all the text-types except the Byzantine antedate Origen. That is historical fact. Westcott and Hort, especially the latter, were not quite as conservative as modern conservative evangelicals. Both made some statements I regret. Nevertheless it is difficult to find a first-rate turn-of-the-century commentary on John's Gospel more conservative than that of Westcott. And his little book entitled *The Revelation of the Father: Short Lectures on the Titles of the Lord in the Gospel of St. John*[43] is superb. Can we not recognize the contributions of such men without writing them off?

What shall we say too about the vast majority of evangelical scholars, including men in whom were found the utmost piety and fidelity to the Word along with scholarship second to none? These men hold that in the basic textual theory Westcott and Hort were right, and that the church stands greatly in their debt. A conservative like Samuel P. Tregelles anticipated Westcott and Hort and their work,[44] and a conservative like Warfield confirmed that work.

42. R. C. Starr, *Is Your Bible* Really *the Word of God?* (Cambridge, Mass.: Cornerstone Baptist Church, n.d.), p. 20.

43. London: Macmillan, 1884.

44. The most recent article on him is the excellent piece by Timothy C. F. Stunt, "Some Unpublished Letters of S. P. Tregelles Relating to the Codex Sinaiticus," *EQ* 48 (1976): 15-26.

I have tried to write this volume without heat or rancor, but I confess I must either laugh or weep when I read merciless diatribes that speak of "apostate texts"; or that "many of our good, fundamental ministers of the gospel, have been caught in the Satanic 'Religious Trap,'" i.e., the idea that there are better manuscripts than those used in the translation of the King James Bible in 1611";[45] or that "even Dr. C. I. Scofield was brainwashed" because he omits Acts 8:37;[46] or that "the orthodox view of the New Testament text" is the one that believes divine providence has stamped the majority text with special approval.[47]

I am upset too by arguments that leap from fourteenth- and fifteenth-century attacks on the Bible per se, to the theory of Westcott and Hort, in order to tar the latter with the brush of the former. I am upset by arguments that take the worst examples of loose paraphrasing in the *Living Bible* and on that basis attack all modern versions. I am equally upset by the sloppiness or the lack of integrity found in arguments that cite authorities like Warfield and Robertson in favor of an inspired and infallible Bible, and then plunge into a defense of the Byzantine tradition in such a fashion as to give the erroneous impression that these men defended the TR. To cite one example: In *Which Bible?* David Otis Fuller, immediately after concluding an argument in favor of the Byzantine text, cites Montgomery's remarks concerning the authenticity and general integrity of the books of the New Testament, as those remarks appear in his *The Suicide of Modern Theology*.[48]

The uninformed reader might well be pardoned if he mistakenly thought that Montgomery favors the TR. As far as I know, he does not. Then Yigael Yadin is cited in his remarks concerning the Masada discoveries. The scrolls found correspond "almost exactly" to the text of the biblical books we use

45. Ray, *God Wrote Only One Bible*, p. 91.

46. Ibid., p. 105.

47. Edward F. Hills, "The Magnificent Burgon," in *Which Bible?*, ed. David Otis Fuller, p. 104.

48. "Why This Book?," in *Which Bible?*, ed. David Otis Fuller, p. 8; *The Suicide of Christian Theology* (Minneapolis: Bethany Fellowship, 1970).

today. But Fuller does not point out that only the Old Testament books are in question, not the New Testament books; and Old Testament textual problems have nothing whatever to do with the four familiar text-types with which the New Testament textual critic must busy himself. Again, the uninformed reader might be pardoned if he came away with the impression that Yadin favors Fuller's position. Of course every person who writes very much sometimes conjures up erroneous impressions quite unwittingly; but it troubles me when this sort of argument appears scores of times in *Which Bible?* I am forced to conclude that some of its writers are either extraordinarily imprecise thinkers or simply dishonest; and of course I prefer the former alternative.

I am far from arguing that all defenders of the KJV are equally intolerant. I do not object to vigorous debate and forceful writing. Even those who use the devices outlined here no doubt feel they are doing so in the cause of truth, although there is no doubt in my mind that many of the inquisitors felt the same thing. What I am saying rather is that debate among Christians ought to be characterized by "speaking the truth in love." I confess I am far from certain that anyone who cannot in principle set his "Amen!" to this thirteenth thesis has come to grips with the most rudimentary content of Scripture. This is so regardless of whether he stands in the succession of the TR or in the succession of an eclectic text.

I am reminded of this poem:

> *Zeal is that pure and heavenly flame*
> *The fire of love supplies;*
> *While that which often bears the name*
> *Is self in a disguise.*

> *True zeal is merciful and mild,*
> *Can pity and forbear:*
> *The false is headstrong, fierce and wild,*
> *And breathes revenge and war.*

> *While zeal for truth the Christian warms,*
> *He knows the worth of peace;*
> *But self contends for names and forms,*
> *Its party to increase.*

The author of these lines is not usually thought of as an apostate or a bleeding-heart liberal. His name is John Newton (1725–1807).

Thesis 14: *Adoption of the TR should not be made a criterion of orthodoxy.* I am under no illusions that this book will persuade all defenders of the TR that they are mistaken. Granted, then, that there will continue to be honest disagreement among us on this textual matter, should either side make its position a criterion of orthodoxy?

I know of no local church that excludes users of the KJV; I know of quite a few that exclude, or try to exclude, users of anything else. Thus even where such churches have not made the adoption of the TR a creedal matter by writing it into their articles of faith or their constitutions, they sometimes begin to act as if they had. An unwritten oral code begins to function in the same way as the written code; and adoption of the TR becomes a criterion of orthodoxy. I would like to think that even if this little book does not convince all who read it that the TR is not the best text, that at least it will persuade a few more that adoption of the TR should not be permitted to function as a binding creedal statement.

Of course some churches and individuals who insist on the KJV do so for nontextual reasons. These nontextual matters deserve careful attention; and it is with them that part 2 of this volume is concerned.

PART 2

Nontextual Questions

CHAPTER 8

Preliminary Considerations

Several preliminary observations may help to dissolve potential misunderstandings.

First, the textual matters I have dealt with concern only the New Testament. The reasons for this are twofold. (1) The defenders of the TR do not usually discuss Old Testament textual problems, and this book is largely a rebuttal. (2) There has not yet occurred as decided a shift in textual tradition in Old Testament studies as took place in New Testament studies almost one hundred years ago. Nevertheless the discovery of the Dead Sea Scrolls provides us with manuscripts of Old Testament books almost one thousand years older than anything previously known. New targums (ancient Aramaic paraphrases) have been discovered. Advances have been made in Semitic lexicography, although certainly it is true that what is sometimes taken as a major advance proves chimerical on the long haul. Septuagintal studies have been gaining momentum.

These developments have not, by and large, prompted scholars to abandon the standard Masoretic text. Minor changes have been made here and there as new readings have come to light;[1] but there is little doubt that the Masoretes and the Jews before and after them were generally more faithful copyists than their Christian counterparts. What has developed, however, is an entire school of thought concerning the textual developments of the Old Testament biblical text. This school is connected with the names of Frank Moore Cross and his pupils,[2] and I think it could become extremely influential. For an able reply, written by an evangelical who is a member of the Tyndale Fellowship for Biblical Research, one might profitably consult the recent article by D. W. Gooding.[3]

I mention these points because I think exclusive focus on New Testament textual-critical problems is symptomatic of (a) a tendency to expend apologetic energy on faddish targets and (b) the very real danger of ignoring other pressing problems that in the long run could prove far more inimical to the church of Jesus Christ than the ones currently drawing a lot of fire from certain quarters.

Second, not all modern translations and paraphrases should be lumped together. The *Living Bible* (LB) really should not be compared with the *New American Standard Bible* (NASB) or the NIV.

Third, it is methodologically indefensible to hunt for the half-dozen worst mistakes or lapses in judgment in a particular translation, and on that basis write off the whole translation. If that method were applied to the KJV, it too would be written off.

Fourth, it follows that no translation is perfect. No translation has *ever* been perfect. Words in different languages and cultures have various shades of meaning. Even when two words

1. For a few easy examples, cf. F. F. Bruce, *Second Thoughts on the Dead Sea Scrolls,* 2d ed. (Grand Rapids: Eerdmans, 1964), pp. 61–69.

2. The most recent work to come from this school is Frank Moore Cross and Shemaryahu Talmon, eds., *Qumran and the History of the Biblical Text* (Cambridge, Mass.: Harvard University, 1975), a collection of the most significant essays published in the last three decades. For a much briefer description of the position of this school, cf. Ralph W. Klein, *Textual Criticism of the Old Testament: The Septuagint After Qumran* (Philadelphia: Fortress, 1974).

3. "A Recent Popularization of Professor F. M. Cross' Theories on the Text of the Old Testament," *TB* 26 (1975): 113–32.

are very close, their semantic overlap is seldom if ever perfect. From language to language, idioms differ, syntax differs, sentence length differs. The stylistic devices used to indicate intensity of emotion are not the same. Poetical standards differ. Words and phrases change their meaning with time. On top of all this, old-fashioned human fallacy intrudes again and again, and just as there is no *biblical* reason for thinking a particular text-type necessarily bears divine approval, so there is no *biblical* reason for thinking a particular translation necessarily bears divine approval.

Fifth, the people who support the KJV for the nontextual reasons I am about to enumerate do not all share the same perspective. Some have already rejected everything but the KJV on textual grounds; that is, they have adopted the TR. The nontextual reasons for defending the KJV, in their view, merely multiply the evidence in favor of the long established version. Others recognize that the textual arguments in favor of the TR are far from convincing, yet they defend the use of the KJV on other grounds.[4] In my judgment the latter are generally more careful in their arguments than most of the former, who seldom even try to attain methodological objectivity. Still others reject the textual reasons for clinging to the TR and find most of the nontextual reasons equally inadequate, yet stand by the KJV for a variety of deeply felt personal reasons: they have used it for fifty years, they have memorized much of it, they love its sonorous cadences. For these people I have the utmost patience and respect, because despite their deep emotional and historical attachment to the KJV, they have preserved a carefulness in debate and a concern for truth that enables them to distinguish a good argument from a bad one.

Sixth, although I am about to defend some modern translations, I would certainly not endorse all of them. I have published a fairly negative judgment on the New English Bible.[5] My students will cheerfully report my negative reaction to the LB. Yet even here one must be careful about being fair. Al-

4. E.g., Iain Murray, "Which Version? A Continuing Debate . . . ," *BanT*, no. 157 (1976): 24–36.

5. "The New English Bible: An Evaluation," *NJT* 1 (1972): 3–14.

though I distrust its looseness, dislike its theological slanting of the evidence (for examples, it is pro Arminianism and pro Dispensationalism, whatever the merits or demerits of these systems), I confess I know many people who first began to read the Bible with interest and diligence once they were exposed to the LB. Many of them left the LB behind once they got into serious Bible study; but the fact remains that the LB was, for them, the first step. Therefore although I myself have little time for the LB and would certainly question the judgment of any pastor or church that adopted it as their Bible for public reading, preaching, teaching, and so forth, nevertheless I would not want to align myself with the intemperate language (not to mention the many factual errors) of some of its most prominent critics.[6]

I have also gone on record in favor of the NIV.[7] In what follows, the versions to which I shall largely restrict myself are the KJV, the NASB, and the NIV.[8] At this writing, only the New Testament plus the books of Isaiah and Daniel have appeared in the NIV; so I shall largely restrict myself to the New Testament. I am sorely tempted to comment on the complete TEV, which put in an appearance recently: but unless I miss my guess, on the long haul it is unlikely to find a large place among evangelicals.[9]

6. I am thinking in particular of the work by Gene Nowlin, *The Paraphrased Perversion of the Bible* (Collingwood, N.J.: The Bible for Today, 1974).

7. *NJT* 4 (1975): 89-93; and elsewhere.

8. For an excellent survey of the most important English versions, cf. Sakae Kubo and Walter Specht, *So Many Versions? Twentieth Century English Versions of the Bible* (Grand Rapids: Zondervan, 1975), to which I have already referred.

9. Cf. the careful review by Ronald F. Youngblood, "Good News for Modern Man: Becoming a Bible," *CT*, 8 October 1976, pp. 16-19.

CHAPTER 9

Some Thoughts on Translating Scripture

In what follows I list the common arguments in favor of retaining the KJV and then seek to answer them. The first takes pride of place because it is by far the most important.

Argument 1: Some hold that, textual questions aside, the KJV is a more accurate translation than its modern counterparts.

This is an extremely difficult question, one that could easily call forth several books.[1] I shall offer a few brief observations that may help to eliminate false arguments and provide some material for fresh reflection.

Anyone who knows two or more modern languages well recognizes how difficult it is to translate material from one to the other in such a way that the material sounds as natural in the receptor language as it does in the donor language, and with the meaning and nuances preserved intact. In English-speaking Canada we speak of the "provincial legislatures." French-speaking Quebec, however, abandoned the French ad-

---

1. John Beekman and John Callow, *Translating the Word of God* (Grand Rapids: Zondervan, 1974), is worth reading; and at a more advanced level Eugene A. Nida and Charles R. Taber, *The Theory and Practice of Translation* (Leiden: Brill, 1964).

jective "provinciale" some years ago, less out of perversity than out of dislike for the nuance carried by the French word. To a French-speaking person the word means "provincial" in an older sense, akin to rural, rustic, even narrow. I do not think such thoughts come to mind when we say "provincial legislature" in English.

Again, to take up an argument I have used elsewhere, I might feel a little hoarse and remark, "I have a frog in my throat." A French-speaking person might speak of the cat in his throat. Of course idiomatic translation would substitute one idiom for the other. This might well be done without loss. But suppose you were translating the French idiom into English and discovered that the former has a nuance quite absent in the latter? Suppose the French word *chat* ("cat") had deep symbolic theological significance: how then should the French sentence be translated into English? Either you will preserve the symbolic content of the noun *cat* (if the reader is sufficiently informed to catch it!) and sacrifice the fluent idiom, giving the erroneous impression that the original was forced, awkward, or heavy; or you will preserve the idiom and sacrifice the symbolic content. As a translator you must choose; you cannot preserve both. And some critics will chew you out no matter what you do. Moreover, if you then have to preach on this text to an English-speaking audience, ideally you, the preacher, should understand enough of the language behind the English version to explain what is going on. If the English has retained "cat," you must explain how easy an idiom this is in French, quite equivalent to our "frog" idiom. If the English has retained the idiom and sacrificed the word, then you must explain the deeper symbolic meaning preserved in the French original.

For such reasons as these we must seek to train pastors to become familiar with the Hebrew and Greek texts.

Consider another example. In German a person might ask the question, "Haben Sie nichts gefunden?" Painfully literally translated, this might be rendered, "Have you nothing found?" Of course German syntax differs from English syntax. A more fluent translation might be, "Haven't you found anything?" The English negates the verb; the German negates the direct object. To translate the German sentence by "Have you found nothing?" will not do:[2] this English sentence invites a response affirming that, yes, something or other has been found; whereas the German, like the English "Haven't you found anything?," does not expect an affirmative response. Of course in certain circumstances, the same German sentence might better be translated, "Didn't you find anything?"—although this might sometimes correspond to "Fanden Sie nichts?"

There is more. The German word for "you" in both sentences is "Sie." The capital letter with which it begins, of course, represents a different orthography from the English. Moreover, this German "you" might be construed as a plural; but if it refers to a single person, then the person thus addressed is certainly of an equal or higher station in life than the speaker; or perhaps he is a total stranger to him. How are you going to get across all that in English?

These three examples, one of which deals with words and their semantic ranges, another with idioms, and a third with syntax and orthography, are very simple indeed. Problems of this type can be far more difficult. In any case they are certainly more difficult when the donor language is two thousand or more years old!

What then is the difference between a "literal" translation and a paraphrase? We might all agree that the NASB is a literal translation and the LB a paraphrase: the two types seem identifiable enough in their extreme forms. But precisely where is the dividing line between the two?

In point of fact, there isn't one. There is a spectrum, a gradation. To compare examples from either end of the spectrum makes differences stand out; but as we approach the center, there is no rigid pattern, no indisputable step that signals the crossing of the line from "literal" translation to paraphrase. And even "literal" I have enclosed in quotation marks because the most literal of translations has to decide what word

2. It is possible to translate the German question by, "Have you found nothing?" (in which case there is only a change in word order); but this presupposes that the German word *nichts* has been underlined, italicized, or otherwise stressed.

best suits the original, make decisions about idioms, search out the appropriate syntax in the receptor language. At all of these steps, there are dangers lurking everywhere for the unwary or the unskilled.

In pointing these things out, I do not mean to encourage such skepticism for our translations (whether KJV or NIV or any other) that henceforth they will be regarded with profound suspicion. Rather, I am opposing the simplistic cast of mind that makes rigid distinctions between a "literal" translation and a "loose" translation, or between a translation and a paraphrase. In thousands of instances, the person who translates the New Testament from Greek into some other language must make decisions that some with equal knowledge may contest, or which involve his understanding of what the text means. Translation is not a purely mechanical process. In a paraphrase from the extreme end of the spectrum, attention is focused on the drift of what a passage means; but even in the most "literal" of translations, the translator must on occasion make decisions as to the meaning of a passage. Or if he rightly understands the meaning, he may nevertheless be forced to choose among several options in the receptor language, all of which leave something to be desired.

The recognition that such things are true, even basic, might evoke a little more caution than is exhibited in one advertisement for an *Interlinear Greek Textus Receptus*. The blurb tells us: "Literal English words appear between the lines, and under each Greek word, making it possible for *anyone* to make an accurate check on all new Bible Versions. Many hard-to-understand verses are made clear by this more literal translation. *It is not necessary to understand Greek, in order to receive help from this book.*"[3]

The book whose back cover contains this advertisement also contains the Greek alphabet and a brief guide to finding one's way around Robert Young's *Analytical Concordance*.[4] I applaud every effort to encourage people to read the New Tes-

---

3. Printed on the back of Jasper James Ray, *God Wrote Only One Bible* (Junction City, Oreg.: Eye Opener, 1970).

4. Ibid., p. 111.

tament in Greek, but I deplore the suggestion that the ability to look up a few words makes one an expert. I have heard pastors with two or three years of Greek behind them (and who therefore should have known better) explain to their congregations what a certain Greek word *means* by citing all the entries in some lexicon and applying *each one* to the text at hand. People with a knowledge of no more than the Greek alphabet are going to make even more mistakes. If we are to teach Greek and Hebrew — and we must! — then let us also teach syntax, idiom, and at least the rudiments of linguistic analysis.

Although there is a danger in repetition, I must say again that all translations are not of equivalent value or accuracy. Just where one places oneself on the spectrum from "literal" translation to loose paraphrase does indeed make a difference. And it is no doubt true that the closer one stands to the "loose" end, the greater the chances of subjective bias. Some modern translations certainly reflect the modernistic presuppositions of their translators from time to time. But just as it is possible to be too loose, it is possible to be too literal. My chief complaint with the NASB, for example, is that it tries so hard to reflect the underlying Greek, Hebrew, and Aramaic that it often resorts to awkward English or unnecessarily stylized English. It attempts to render Greek imperfects consistently by English imperfects, a procedure not only insensitive to the flexibility of Greek tenses but even more insensitive to English idiom. This fault is especially noticeable in the Gospels. The KJV too falls under the condemnation of being too literal at certain points. I shall provide examples a little further on. This is one of the errors that the translators of the NIV, all of whom were selected because of both their scholarship and their evangelical commitment, seek to minimize.

In a recent article Iain Murray, editor of *The Banner of Truth,* defended the KJV against the NIV largely on the ground that the former attempted a more literal translation, and this, he alleged, was more in keeping with the doctrine of inspiration.[5] It is a fair assessment, I think, that says the KJV is

5. Iain Murray, "Which Version? A Continuing Debate . . .," *BanT,* no. 157 (1976): 31–32. For example, he says, "God's Word, *correctly translated*

more literal than the NIV, although, as I have indicated, I doubt very much if that should always be taken as a compliment. But why a literal translation is necessarily more in keeping with the doctrine of verbal inspiration, I am quite at a loss to know. For example, if I may refer again to an illustration I have just used, to translate "Haben Sie nichts gefunden?" by "Have you nothing found?" would scarcely be more honoring to the German author than "Haven't you found anything?," even though the latter translation is certainly less literal than the former. The Holy Spirit who inspired the words of Scripture equally inspired the syntax and the idioms. Ultimately what we want of a translation is a rendering that means what the original means, both in denotation and connotation. Even if one objects to Eugene A. Nida's[6] famous expression, "dynamic equivalent," because it can lead to all sorts of freedoms with respect to the translation, it ought to be obvious that to some extent *every* translation, from *anywhere* on the spectrum, is necessarily involved again and again with finding the "dynamic equivalent." Just as no translation is perfect, so also no translation is perfectly objective. The question to ask of any particular rendering is simply this: Is this the best possible translation of the passage, taking into account the meaning of the words of both languages, their syntax, their idioms, how this rendering is understood as compared with how a reader of the original text would understand what he read (and even that is a tricky test), and so forth.

Murray does not accept the TR as the best text, if one may judge by the articles published in the *Banner*.[7] Therefore his defense of the KJV is based not on textual arguments but on

---

[italics mine], is infallible, our interpretation of it is not." True enough: but no translation could ever be infallibly correct unless it were guided by the same Spirit, with the same degree of supervision, as was the writing of the inspired autographs. Every effort at translation entails some interpretation on the part of the translator.

6. Nida is one of the world's most prominent and capable Bible translators and linguistic experts. Long associated with the American Bible Society and the United Bible Societies, he has published many books. His articles appear regularly in the journal literature, perhaps most frequently in *BT*.

7. Donald MacLeod, "The Bible and Textual Criticism," *BanT*, no. 111 (1972): 12–26; and Murray, "Which Version?"

questions of translation. Yet if he wants a very literal translation and does not find the NIV suitable in this regard, why does he not adopt the NASB? In my judgment the NASB is even more literal than the KJV; and it has the added advantage that it does not rest on an inferior text, one, in fact, that accepts readings attested in no Greek manuscript whatsoever. I would have thought this should be of more than incidental concern to anyone committed to accuracy and literalness. I suspect that in some instances at least (although I would not be prepared to say it was so in the case of Murray, whom I have not had the pleasure of meeting) the real reason for retaining the KJV has more to do with argument 7 (below) than with anything else.

I must say a further word about words. In the journal from Bob Jones University, the president, Bob Jones III, in expounding Psalm 119:103, "How sweet are thy words unto my taste!," points out that what is sweet is nothing less than God's words: certainly not "the words of a man's paraphrase."[8] His exegesis is correct: that is what the text says. However, when Jones, on the basis of this passage, then proceeds to distinguish between paraphrases and translations, and claims that only the latter contain God's words, I fear he is playing loose with the text. To the psalmist God's words were in Hebrew; and no matter how careful, how literal the translation of those words into English, the result is still English words. And the semantic range of the English word will seldom if ever correspond exactly to the semantic range of the Hebrew word (or expression!) that underlies it.

Take, for example, the Hebrew word *nephesh*. It can mean "soul, heart, life, man, beast"; it sometimes takes the place of a pronoun (for example, "herself" in Isa. 5:14 KJV); and if idioms are considered, it can mean "neck, throat, and desire."[9] The Hebrew word *ruach*, often translated "spirit," has an even wider semantic range.[10]

8. "O How I Love Thy Law!," *Biblical Viewpoint* 10 (1976): 97.

9. Cf. the brief study by Heber F. Peacock, "Translating the Word for 'Soul' in the Old Testament," *BT* 27 (1976): 216–19.

10. Cf. Norman H. Snaith, *The Distinctive Ideas of the Old Testament* (Philadelphia: Westminster, 1946), pp. 143–58.

The expression *mē genoito* is a fairly common Pauline locution. The KJV translates it "God forbid," even though God is not mentioned. More literally rendered, it becomes "May it not be"; but who talks English like that today? The NIV favors expressions like "Not at all!" (Rom. 3:4), "Never!" (I Cor. 6:15), and the like, which catch it perfectly.

Modern versions are much criticized for translating *monogenēs* by "only," "unique," "one and only," and the like, instead of KJV's "only begotten." In so doing they are accused of detracting from Jesus' virgin birth. I do not think the doctrine of the virgin birth hangs on one word, so if lexical evidence points to the rendering of the modern versions, I do not feel threatened. As the word was used in documents approximately contemporaneous with the New Testament, it did not have the meaning "only begotten." In fact it became almost a synonym for *agapētos*, "beloved." This is demonstrable even from the evidence of the New Testament itself. The word appears in Luke 7:12; 8:42; 9:38; John 1:14, 18; 3:16, 18; Hebrews 11:17; and I John 4:9. In all of the references outside the Johannine corpus, the word is applied to persons other than Jesus. In none of the Lucan passages does the KJV find it necessary to translate it by "only begotten." That the word can mean a little more than "only" is made clear from its use in Hebrews 11:17. There, Isaac is called Abraham's *monogenēs* son. Now, clearly, Isaac was not Abraham's "only begotten" son, despite the KJV, for Abraham fathered Ishmael and others. Equally clearly, Isaac was not Abraham's "one and only son," despite the NIV. Isaac was Abraham's special son, his unique son, his beloved son. And in the Lucan passages that same meaning always fits admirably, although "only" is possible. In the Johannine passages, I suspect the meaning is "unique" or "unique and beloved," for John lays repeated emphasis on the fact that, although believers become God's children, Jesus alone is son in the special sense. In Johannine vocabulary others become *ta tekna* (the children) of God; Jesus alone is *ho huios* (the son)—indeed, the beloved son, because He always does what is pleasing in the Father's sight (John 8:28–29). Modern translations like the NIV are not by their rendering of *monogenēs* reflecting an apostate desire to meddle with the

Word of God. Rather, they are at this point more accurate than the KJV. These facts have been documented repeatedly,[11] and so it is disappointing to face the same misinformed charges at this late date.

A few examples of instances where the KJV is so literal as to be either unnecessarily obscure or actually misleading may serve to tie together the argument to this point. In Galatians 5:5 the KJV reads, "For we through the Spirit wait for the hope of righteousness by faith." The NIV of the same passage reads, "But by faith we eagerly await through the Spirit the righteousness for which we hope." Transliterated, the Greek reads, *hēmeis gar pneumati ek pisteōs elpida dikaiosunēs apekdechometha.* It is highly likely that both "by faith" and "through the Spirit" modify the verb; and therefore the KJV's placement of "by faith" is potentially misleading. The NIV replaces "wait for" with "eagerly await," a faithful rendering of the heightened compound verb. But the greatest difference is the change from "the hope of righteousness" (KJV) to "the righteousness for which we hope" (NIV). The latter is superior, even if less literal. The Greek genitive is objective: the thing hoped for, and thus the thing eagerly awaited, is righteousness. The KJV scarcely makes that clear; the NIV has it exactly.

In Romans 12:16 the KJV has: "Be of the same mind one toward another. Mind not high things, but condescend to men of low estate. Be not wise in your own conceits." The NIV reads: "Live in harmony with one another. Do not be proud, but be willing to associate with people of low position [footnote: Or "willing to do menial work"]. Do not be conceited." I would be prepared to argue that the first and third clauses of the NIV's rendering are superior to the analogous clauses of the KJV; but it is the second clause that calls for attention at the moment. The Greek is actually a hanging-sentence fragment; both the KJV and NIV have made a sentence out of it. "Mind not high things" is more literal; but in the twentieth century that sounds like "Don't pay attention to high and noble thoughts (or to noble or prestigious things?)." The NIV's

---

11. E.g., Dale Moody, " 'God's Only Son': The Translation of John 3:16 in the Revised Standard Version," *JBL* 72 (1953): 213–19.

"Do not be proud" is not quite as literal, but it translates the meaning with far greater accuracy. The KJV tells us to "condescend to men of low estate." To the modern ear that sounds "condescending" in a way not suggested by the Greek text. The NIV is again superior.

In III John 2 we read these words in the KJV: "Beloved, I wish above all things that thou mayest prosper and be in health, even as thy soul prospereth." The NIV reads, "Dear friend, I pray that you may enjoy good health and that all may go well with you, even as your soul is getting along well." The NIV's "I pray" is a better rendering of *euchomai* than the KJV's "I wish." But the most important difference between the two English translations is this: the KJV renders the Greek *peri pantōn* as "above all else," construing it with the finite verb to mean that John wishes for this particular thing more than he wishes for anything else; whereas the NIV construes the same phrase with the infinitive *eudousthai* to produce the clause, "and that all may go well with you." The KJV has missed the point of the Greek text by pedantically following the Greek word order. III John contains two or three such major gaffes in verses 6 and 7.[12]

In Luke 17:11 the KJV reads, "And it came to pass, as he went to Jerusalem, that he passed through the midst of Samaria and Galilee." Contrast the NIV: "Now on his way to Jerusalem, Jesus traveled along the border between Samaria and Galilee." The reference to "the border" in the latter depends in part on a variant reading, and at the moment I am not concerned with textual problems. Right at the beginning of the verse, however, the KJV translates the Greek *kai egeneto* as "And it came to pass." The Greek is actually an imitation of a common Hebrew idiom that serves as a connective, nothing more. The NIV preserves the same effect, and yet retains contemporaneity, by translating less literally but perhaps even more accurately, "Now . . ."

---

12. A careful check on any exegetical commentary will make this clear. For instance, cf. John R. W. Stott, *The Epistles of John: An Introduction and Commentary*, TNTC (Grand Rapids: Eerdmans, 1964).

I could provide hundreds and hundreds of such examples; but these will suffice. I have purposely chosen passages where a mininum of doctrinal content is at stake in order to make the point in a minimally charged atmosphere.

A related problem clamors for attention. The translators of the KJV, as accomplished as they were, were totally unaware of the differences between Hellenistic (or Koine) Greek and the classical (usually Attic) Greek of earlier centuries. The relevant manuscripts had not yet been discovered. As late as 1886 Joseph Henry Thayer could list 767 distinctively "New Testament" words with no parallels in any known Greek literature. The list is now considerably under 50 and still shrinking. Moreover in 1611 translators followed the syntax of classical Greek; but now we know that the Greek of the New Testament corresponds syntactically to Hellenistic Greek. This makes a tremendous difference in, for example, the connecting phrases of the Johannine epistles. Moreover some words and idioms had changed their meaning over the centuries, and the New Testament writers used the language of their times. For example, the Holy Spirit is said to be an *arrabōn* (II Cor. 1:22; 5:5; Eph. 1:14). The KJV translates the word as "earnest" or "guarantee." The former word probably conveys nothing to most contemporary readers of the KJV, because they are unaware of the obsolete expression "earnest money." However, the Greek word has been found in business records preserved among the secular papyri to designate a "down payment." That is indeed what Paul means: the Holy Spirit is the down payment of our salvation, the full payment of which awaits the consummation. Many similar examples could be added.[13]

Another problem affecting the accuracy of translation has recently been raised. One or two have pointed out that the KJV tends to preserve the sentence length of the Greek text, whereas the NIV chops up the longer passages.[14] Some feel it is

---

13. Cf. George E. Ladd, *The New Testament and Criticism* (Grand Rapids: Eerdmans, 1967), pp. 89ff. More-advanced students will want to study C. F. D. Moule, *An Idiom Book of New Testament Greek,* 2d ed. (Cambridge: University Press, 1959).

14. E.g., compare the two translations at Eph. 1:3ff.

more accurate to preserve the greater length of the sentences; for after all, English itself may revert to the style of the Puritans in this regard.[15] Part of this warning is, I think, most salutary; there is certainly a danger in trying to concoct a translation that is simpler than the Greek text itself![16] Nevertheless we must distinguish between difficulties imposed by the content and style of the original material, and difficulties imposed by poor translation. It is good Greek to write long sentences laced with subordinate clauses and garnished with participles. By contrast, even the long sentences of the Puritans often tend to coordinate clauses where the Greek would subordinate them, simply because that was the way English was then written. Nowadays English is written with shorter sentences; so if we are translating the Word of God into the language of the people, we will use shorter sentences. To retain the KJV because English may return to long sentences is a counsel of despair. If we have to wait another three hundred years for this to occur, the KJV will by then have long since vanished, for it would then be more than six hundred years old. There would exist as great a distance between the English of 1611 and the English of that future age as now exists between Geoffrey Chaucer and ourselves.

Another charge sometimes brought against the NIV is that it plays fast and loose with Greek connectives. I think this charge is very occasionally justified. An example might be John 11:3. Nevertheless two comments may put this criticism in more realistic perspective: (1) Greek tends to use a connective at the head of every sentence unless it wants a specific break. To translate all such connectives literally is poor English, which does not adopt the same stylistic feature. This explains the very high proportion of sentences in the KJV that begin with a conjunction. (2) The semantic range of Greek connec-

---

15. So John Skilton, in a review of the NIV New Testament, *WTJ* 37 (1975): 261-62.

16. Cf. Stephen Neill: "I remember once exploding angrily in the Tamil Bible translation committee, when we had so smoothed out the complex passage Galatians 2:1-10 as to conceal completely the tensions and confusions which underlie the apostle's twisted grammar. This we had no right to do." "Translating the Word of God," *The Churchman* 90 (1976): 287.

tives is far wider than many introductory grammar books admit. For example, one might think of *gar* as meaning "for"; but there are times when smooth, accurate translation might be better served by "but."

I am far from arguing that any translation is perfect. Nevertheless, all things taken together, it is my considered judgment that the NIV New Testament is the best English translation of the Greek Testament now available. It is, of course, still being improved: printing errors are being eliminated, and the senior committee is still receiving suggestions for improving the rendering at any particular point. In this, of course, it is repeating the history of the KJV, which also had to have the worst of its errors weeded out during the early days of its existence.[17]

Argument 2: Some argue that the KJV has withstood 350 years of wear and tear; and it is unlikely therefore that it will be displaced by more recent versions.

The *form* of this argument is singularly unimpressive. It could have been applied to the Latin Vulgate about the time of John Wycliffe (ca. 1320–1384). However, what is most likely *meant* by the argument is that the KJV has demonstrated its superiority by serving as the most important English Bible for 350 years, and this superiority it still retains.

Perhaps it needs to be pointed out that the KJV has not competed against the NASB and NIV for 350 years! The textual question aside, the antiquated language of the KJV is going to become a great deal more antiquated during the next fifty or a hundred years. Unless the Lord comes back first, the KJV will sooner or later pass away as the predominant English version; and I predict it will be sooner rather than later.

Argument 3: It is alleged that the old English forms are more reverent, and sometimes more precise, than their modern equivalents. "Thou" is more respectful than "You," and so forth.

I confess I have difficulty sympathizing with this argument, because I was reared in Quebec. There, French-

17. Cf. F. F. Bruce, *The Books and the Parchments: Some Chapters on the Transmission of the Bible,* 3d ed. (Westwood, N.J.: Revell, 1963), pp. 229–30. Moreover all early editions of the KJV contained the Apocrypha.

speaking evangelicals address God as "tu," the familiar form of "you," leaving the most respectful "vous" to the high Roman Catholics. Clearly, what is reverent and respectful to one group is stuffy and artificial to another; what is irreverent and disrespectful to one group is a sign of personal relationship and boldness of access to another.

In the first century, books written for the literati were still written in Attic Greek. Is there something to be learned from the fact that the New Testament documents were written by men who, moved by the Holy Spirit, chose rather the colloquial Hellenistic Greek?

Moreover, there is a decreasing number of people today who can read Elizabethan English and readily understand it. The person brought up on the KJV knows that "deny" in Matthew 26:34 really means "disown"; that *"Suffer* little children . . ." really means to permit them to come; that "prevent" in I Thessalonians 4:15 really means "precede." But not many others do. Is not the NIV's rendering of Romans 1:28 far less mysterious than that of the KJV? The latter reads: "And even as they did not like to retain God in their knowledge, God gave them over to a reprobate mind, to do those things which are not convenient." The NIV reads: "Furthermore, since they did not think it worthwhile to retain the knowledge of God, he gave them over to a depraved mind, to do what ought not to be done." Or compare II Corinthians 8:1 in the two versions: "Moreover, brethren, we do you to wit of the grace of God bestowed on the churches of Macedonia" (KJV); "And now, brothers, we want you to know about the grace that God has given the Macedonian churches." How many will read, "Thou shalt destroy them that speak leasing" (Ps. 5:6), and know it is talking about liars?

It is true that Elizabethan English is more precise than modern English in its use of pronouns. Nevertheless I confess that, as a preacher, I would rather specify the exact meaning of the odd ambiguous pronoun now and then, than explain all the archaisms in the text of the KJV. When it is argued that the Hebrew and Greek use singular forms, and that therefore we must do likewise,[18] I confess I cannot agree. Such an argument, pressed home, would mean we could only address God, or talk about revealed truth, in Hebrew, Aramaic, and Greek. When I pray to God using *you*, I am certainly addressing Him in the singular; the pronoun includes the singular meaning in its semantic range. Conversely, given the appropriate idiom, singular forms can bear plural significance; note the interchange of plural and singular in the Greek text of II John as the recipients of the letter are addressed as individuals or under the singular figure of a lady.

Argument 4: Some argue on other grounds that the KJV preserves a translation that honors the Lord Jesus more than its rivals do. For example, the KJV preserves "Lord" and "Christ" around "Jesus" more often than other translations do.

Of course this is in part a textual question. Apart from that, however, it is important to realize that even in the KJV, the Gospels speak of "Jesus" absolutely considerably more often than they speak of the "Lord Jesus," "Jesus Christ," or the "Lord Jesus Christ." I cannot see where the Scriptures teach that one designation is more reverent than another. I suspect such value judgments spring more from popular piety than from the Word of God.

Meanwhile it is worth noting that the KJV refers to the Holy Spirit as "itself" (Rom. 8:26), apparently because it is translating too literally: the Greek word is neuter. Why does no one complain about the irreverence of the KJV in referring to the Holy Spirit as "it"?

Argument 5: Many argue for the retention of the KJV because it is easy to memorize, and abandoning it too often means abandoning the attempt to memorize God's Word.

This is a very serious argument. There are really two different elements to it. The first claims, somewhat naively, that the KJV is easier to memorize than others because of its English. There is no basis for such a claim. It often *appears* easier to memorize in those cases in which a person has been brought

---

18. Cf. Arthur W. Kuschke: "We should address God as the Bible does. If we use 'you' we fail to identify God as he has identified himself to us, and as he has required us to worship him." Cited in Murray, "Which Version?," p. 35.

up with it at home and at church. He has imbibed a great deal of it quite unknowingly, and when he comes to memorize it he discovers there are parts of it he already knows.

The second element follows on, and is more serious. When only one translation is used everywhere, for private reading as for corporate worship, some memorizing occurs automatically. Thus if all without exception used only one translation (KJV or otherwise), there would be more memorizing of Scripture. But whether we like it or not, we are, in most areas of the English-speaking world, moving out of that situation. People will have to choose to memorize a particular passage from a particular version. And of course if the argument were pressed to extremes, it would mean we could *never* change to another version, regardless of how archaic the KJV became; for any change is certainly going to involve at least an awkward transition period.

During the past ten or fifteen years I have read quite a few Bible translations right though; and no doubt as a result I have not memorized as much of the KJV as I would otherwise have done. For the past year and a half or so, I have committed myself to memorizing exclusively from the NIV and have tucked a growing number of chapters away in my memory. I think Christians will have to take conscious decisions like that in the years ahead.

Argument 6: The KJV, it is alleged, is particularly suitable for public reading.

Again there are two elements to the argument. The first affirms that the cadence and exalted prose of the KJV make it appropriate as the version to be read from the pulpit. This is really a variation on argument 3. Some modern versions are certainly inappropriate for pulpit use (the LB comes most readily to mind); but I can think of no objection to the NIV.

The second element insists on the importance of corporate reading and responsive reading. Obviously such practices require a uniformly accepted translation. I concur that corporate and responsive readings are highly desirable. However, from a pastoral perspective it is possible to introduce the entire congregation to *one* other version, and over a period of two or three years bring the congregation to the place where it will read corporately on occasion from some version other than the KJV.

Argument 7: Some argue that they like the KJV; and that is all there is to it.

I have enormous respect for this position, especially if it is accompanied by an honest recognition of the general inadequacy of the other arguments in favor of the KJV. I too was brought up on this cherished version; and much of what I have memorized from the Scripture still comes out in that form. My move to other versions was facilitated by two factors not shared by all: (1) I began to rely more and more on the original languages and less and less on the KJV; and (2) for quite a while I moved in student circles.

If a large part of an entire congregation enjoys this deep personal and emotional tie to the KJV, it is certainly the better part of wisdom to tread lightly when it comes to instituting changes. Nevertheless some changes are inevitable. For a start, some of the young people will begin reading modern versions. The congregation should become sufficiently aware of the strengths and weaknesses of various translations that its members do not become defensive and wary, primed to accept every argument in favor of the KJV. If the spiritual leaders endorse only the KJV, and either ban everything else or ignore all other versions in the hope that they will go away, those leaders may rest assured that the younger believers will find their own modern versions. Regrettably, lacking the knowledge that could have promoted the NIV or the NASB, this younger generation will probably opt for the LB. Thus even where a senior saint has a deep emotional commitment to the KJV, he will probably be wise to make himself familiar with the best of the modern versions and to be prepared to recommend one of them to others who may not share his commitment to the KJV.

The plain truth of the matter is that the version that is so cherished among senior saints who have more or less come to terms with Elizabethan English, is obscure, confusing, and sometimes even incomprehensible[19] to many younger or poorly

---

19. I refer to the language, not the content; for the content is always incomprehensible to the man without the Spirit (I Cor. 2:14).

educated Christians. The words of Edwin H. Palmer are not too strong: "Do not give them a loaf of bread, covered with an inedible, impenetrable crust, fossilized by three and a half centuries. Give them the Word of God as fresh and warm and clear as the Holy Spirit gave it to the authors of the Bible. . . . For any preacher or theologian who loves God's Word to allow that Word to go on being misunderstood because of the veneration of an archaic, not-understood version of four centuries ago is inexcusable, and almost unconscionable."[20]

20. "Dear Duncan: About That Review of the NIV . . .," *The Presbyterian Guardian* 44 (1975): 126-27.

Conclusion

In this book I have tried to concern myself with principles. As a result I have indulged in relatively little discussion of specific biblical passages, reserving them primarily for illustration. Had I attempted to touch on all the passages that have been treated in the recent literature on this subject, this little volume would have taken a far different form.

The church of Jesus Christ must constantly pursue reformation. Any body of believers that is bound by its heritage, however splendid that heritage may be, has already begun the drift to heterodoxy. The church *must be being reformed* (however grammatically awkward that may sound). And the sole basis for such information is the Word of God. In the hope that God will again visit His church with renewal and life nurtured by the Scriptures, I applaud every effort to put those Scriptures, in quality vernacular translations, into the hands of men and women everywhere.[1]

---

1. Cf. the Westminster Confession of Faith: "But, because these original tongues are not known to all the people of God, who have right unto, and interest in the Scriptures, and are commanded, in the fear of God, to read and search them, therefore they are to be translated into the vulgar language of every nation unto which they come, that, the Word of God dwelling plenti-

fully in all, they may worship Him in an acceptable manner; and, through patience and comfort of the Scriptures, may have hope" (1:8).

A Critique of *The Identity of the New Testament Text*

Of the books that have been written in defense of a Textus Receptus type of text, perhaps none is more convincing than *The Identity of the New Testament Text*.[1] Written by Wilbur N. Pickering, this little book adopts a line of reasoning quite different from most others that defend its viewpoint. Because of its unique approach to the textual question and because it appeared after most of the preceding pages were written, I have decided to deal with it separately in this appendix.

Pickering has done some hard work. His thesis, in brief, is that eclecticism is not a method to be trusted because there is insufficient evidence that identifiable text-types even existed. The only alternative is to resort to a method of counting manuscripts. It follows inescapably that in those passages where the Byzantine text-type differs from the other text-types, the Byzantine reading will be chosen, for the simple reason that it boasts majority support. Because Pickering does not believe the existence of isolatable text-types has been demonstrated, he prefers to talk about the "majority text" rather than the Byz-

1. Wilbur N. Pickering, *The Identity of the New Testament Text* (Nashville: Nelson, 1977).

antine tradition or the Byzantine text-type; but his majority text differs from the Byzantine text in concept only, not in substance.

It is worthwhile outlining the book in a little more detail. The book opens with an approving forward written by Zane C. Hodges of Dallas Theological Seminary, where Pickering earned a M.Th. Pickering's first chapter is a brief introduction, which raises questions about the propriety of eclecticism as a method and cites a couple of scholars who have voiced their doubts about our ability to achieve certainty concerning the New Testament text. The second chapter marshalls evidence against eclecticism, culled from the writings of those who still use it but who are dissatisfied with it. Chapter 3 offers a thumbnail sketch of the rise of the theory of B. F. Westcott and F. J. A. Hort, and chapter 4 a critical evaluation. Pickering seeks to show that Hort was prejudiced against the Byzantine text-type from the beginning of his work, and that his opinions, far from being the result of careful study, were what prompted the work. Hort, Pickering alleges, succeeded in overthrowing the supremacy of the Byzantine tradition by constructing his genealogical theory. Once accepted, the theory insists that manuscripts relating to one text-type can together offer only one vote for a particular reading. Conversely, two or three manuscripts of different genealogy, of different text-type, provide two or three independent votes. Thus in principle a small number of manuscripts attesting a particular reading could be accepted above a large number of manuscripts that support some other reading. Pickering, however, calls the entire genealogical principle into question. He refers to a number of important studies that could not detect clear genealogical relationships among manuscripts of the Byzantine tradition. More important, many of the ante-Nicene witnesses, including the papyri, are so "mixed" in the type of text they reflect that notable textual critics have raised the question whether "text-type" in the Westcott-Hort sense is a meaningful expression. Pickering has done textual critics a favor by pulling some of this material together.

Chapter 4 also deals with a host of lesser questions that rise out of the Westcott-Hort theory. Pickering cites studies that find evidence of Byzantine readings in the early fathers, and other studies that affirm an early date for the Syriac Peshitta (which reflects Byzantine readings) or that cast doubt on the established principles of textual citicism. He points out that few scholars today treat the Byzantine text-type as if it were a recension; and if not a late recension, as Westcott and Hort proposed, then how did it originate?

That brings us to a crucial question, the one that occupies Pickering's attention in the fifth chapter. Regardless of what textual-critical theory is adopted, that theory must be held in conjunction with a related and believable history of the text. If the Byzantine tradition did not arise as a late recension (as Westcott and Hort suggested), then how are we to account for it? Pickering offers an alternative textual history, one that projects the majority text (the Byzantine text-type) back to the earliest period. Deviations from this must be dismissed as early aberrations, weeded out in the passage of time.

In the sixth chapter Pickering answers various potential objections to his reconstruction. Why, for example, are there no early Byzantine manuscripts? Because, says Pickering, they wore out. Should not manuscripts be weighed, not counted? Pickering thinks counting is to be preferred because he has already dispensed with the genealogical principle — at least to his own satisfaction. Chapter 7 affords Pickering the opportunity of formulating his thesis in terms of John W. Burgon's old "Notes of Truth," a summary of textual-critical principles Pickering would approve of over against currently adopted textual-critical principles. The last chapter, the eighth, offers a brief conclusion.

The book includes three appendices. The first relates the doctrine of inspiration to the preservation of the text. Pickering says that the affirmation that "God has preserved the original wording of the New Testament text" is "a statement of faith"; but this acknowledgment of the need for faith is coupled with an insistence that such faith is "an intelligent faith, a faith that accords with the available evidence."[2] The second appendix discusses 7Q5, the manuscript fragment from

2. Ibid., p. 144.

Qumran that the Jesuit scholar José O'Callaghan identified as a piece of Mark 6:52–53. Pickering feels that published criticism of O'Callaghan's work is ill informed and that O'Callaghan is probably right. The third and by far the longest appendix applies the methods of probability statistics to the history of the text. Here Pickering is drawing on his expertise in linguistics (he is a candidate for a Ph.D. in linguistics from the University of Toronto). This is an original approach to the question; but I shall reserve comment for a few moments.

My criticisms of this book are extensive; but before launching into a few of them, I want to commend Pickering for bringing together the cream of significant studies that cast doubt on the reconstruction offered us by Westcott and Hort, and especially for asking many of the right questions. This said, I fear Pickering's alternative is even more problematic than the theory of Westcott and Hort. The tragedy of Pickering's work, I believe, is that his important and pertinent questions will tend to be overlooked and dismissed by scholars of textual criticism, who will find many reasons to reject his reconstruction and therefore his questions, while many conservative Christians will accept his entire reconstruction without detecting the many underlying questions that will still go unanswered.

Specifically I would venture at least the following criticisms:

First, there is a basic flaw in Pickering's overarching argument. Having demonstrated that text-types are not as sharply delineated as some have thought, he argues that the very concept is misguided and concludes therefore that we must view most manuscripts as independent authorities that ought to be counted, not weighed. Yet at the same time he quite clearly preserves the concept of text-type as applied to the Byzantine tradition, even though he prefers to call it the "majority text." For example, he contends that distinctively Byzantine readings are found in the ante-Nicene fathers, but he admits there is not one examplar of the Byzantine tradition per se from the early period. In fact when he asks why there isn't one, he is reduced to the weak answer that they all wore out. However, whatever the merits of this answer, the fact that he can ask the question indicates that the concept of text-types still occupies a large place in his thinking, at least as far as the Byzantine tradition is concerned. But if that is so, then he ought not reject the genealogical principle so categorically: it sounds too much like simultaneously keeping one's cake and eating it.

What recent studies have shown, I think, is that the four classic text-types are too neatly isolated. Perhaps we are forced to conclude that most early manuscripts are mixes. If so, the boundaries between text-types become hazy, like the change from color to color in a rainbow; but it still does not follow that the concept of text-types is entirely dispensable, any more than we could dispense with the colors of the rainbow, or argue that those colors cannot be distinguished from one another. Perhaps p^{66} presents confusing evidence and therefore lives in the hazy zone; but the evidence from p^{75} is remarkably clear. (Later I shall say more on these papyri.) No doubt the four well-known text-types constitute an inadequate basis that still needs much work; but that distinct types of texts exist cannot be dismissed. If the expression *text-type* refers to neatly isolated types of text, then it may be that the pursuit of text-types is an illusory goal; but if *text-type* simply refers to types of text as indexed by several remarkable extremes, it is hard to see how anyone can deny their existence. Once this point is conceded, it follows that simply counting manuscripts will not prove very helpful. Besides, even if it is premature and sometimes misleading to assign this manuscript or that to a particular text-type, nevertheless a few discrete "families"[3] of texts have been found (for example, the so-called Lake family), demonstrating that genealogical relationships do in fact exist.

On the face of it, because one manuscript was copied from another or from several others, genealogical relationships *must* exist. The only question is whether or not we have identified such relationships, or can identify them. Off the cuff, I suspect we have too often neglected the mobility of the first century. Roman roads and imperial peace meant movement; and just as the overlooking of these factors has contributed to a

---

3. Since the work of E. C. Colwell, most New Testament textual critics have reserved the word *family* for smaller groupings within a particular text-type.

proliferation of theories concerning "Matthean theology" over against the theology of the "Pauline churches" over against the theology of the "Johannine circle," as if the various groups were almost hermetically sealed off from one another, so also I suspect that early textual history involves more borrowing and cross-fertilization than is often recognized. Yet such fluidity does nothing to mitigate against the *principle* of text-types and genealogical relationships.

Second, Pickering's use of the studies by Edward Miller, though challenging, raises more questions than it answers. Miller, posthumous editor to Burgon, compiled from Burgon's notes and his own studies a complete list of Byzantine readings in the ante-Nicene fathers.[4] He discovered that Byzantine readings invariably outnumber readings of other traditions, but in various ratios. This, it is argued, proves the earliness of the Byzantine text-type.

Textual-critical scholars have responded to this in various ways. First of all, detailed critical editions of the fathers had not been prepared in Miller's day. Many Byzantine readings in the late manuscripts of the fathers may well be due to assimilation to the Byzantine text-type in the post-Nicene period. Of course there is a danger of arguing in a circle here; so let us be conservative and suppose that there were but few assimilations. It then follows that many Byzantine readings are found in the ante-Nicene fathers. However, that fact by itself still proves nothing because textual scholars hold that a primary feature of the Byzantine text-type is its tendency to conflate readings. Obviously, then, the elements of the conflation must antedate the conflation itself. The point is that the vast majority of so-called Byzantine readings in the ante-Nicene fathers are also Western or Alexandrian readings. They become *distinctively* Byzantine only by their conflation in individual manuscripts *after* the fourth century has got underway. The question is whether or not the *Byzantine text-type* existed before the fourth century, not whether or not *Byzantine readings* existed before the fourth century. In the absence of any

---

4. Edward Miller, *A Guide to the Textual Criticism of the New Testament* (London: Bell, 1886). Cf. Pickering, *The New Testament Text,* pp. 64ff.

ante-Nicene manuscript boasting Byzantine text-type, Miller — and Pickering — draw outsize conclusions from the patristic evidence.

Pickering rightly points out that the ante-Nicene fathers also contain some uniquely Byzantine readings: that is, readings that are found in no text-type other than Byzantine. There are not many of them, but there are a few. Pickering seems to think that their presence proves the early existence of the Byzantine text-type. Of course it does nothing of the kind. Such purely Byzantine words *may* attest to the ante-Nicene existence of the Byzantine text-type; but other explanations are equally possible. For example, the small number of ante-Nicene witnesses (as compared with the larger number of later manuscripts) is well known, and it is frequently pointed out by Pickering himself. Before the discoveries of the best Western, and especially the Alexandrian, witnesses within the last two centuries, one might have supposed that most of the "Byzantine" words found in the ante-Nicene fathers were purely Byzantine. With the discovery of other witnesses, the number of purely Byzantine readings found in the ante-Nicene fathers was reduced to a minute fraction of the total because more and more "Byzantine" readings were also found to be Western or Alexandrian. Perhaps the discovery of a few more manuscripts will reduce that number yet further.

This of course is the converse of the argument of Edward F. Hills (and of Pickering, who cites him).[5] Hort said that the Byzantine text-type is characterized by late readings, yet Hills contends that only about 10 percent of the Byzantine readings are really late; and with new discoveries, this percentage is still falling. True enough; but with each falling percentage point, the number of purely Byzantine readings found in the ante-Nicene fathers is correspondingly reduced.

What this means is that the patristic evidence is at best ambiguous. In the absence of any ante-Nicene exemplar of the Byzantine text-type, the onus of proof, in my view, still rests with the defenders of the Byzantine tradition.

5. Pickering, *The New Testament Text*, p. 71.

Of course a translation, dated unambiguously early, that clearly boasted the mature Byzantine text-type, would also serve as adequate proof of the early existence of this tradition. That is why the date of the Syriac Peshitta has often been considered important. In point of fact, the textual affinity of the Peshitta to the Byzantine tradition has regularly been overestimated: the close work that has been done on some parts of it (especially Mark and Galatians) reflects Byzantine readings only about 50 percent of the time.[6] In any case, although up until the turn of the century it was almost universally accepted that the Peshitta was a second-century translation, scarcely anyone will defend that position today. As I indicated earlier,[7] F. C. Burkitt convinced almost everyone that it was the fifth-century work of Rabbula of Edessa. Arthur Vööbus disagreed sharply, pointing out a number of instances in which Rabbula's quotations from Scripture are not from the Peshitta but from the Old Syriac. Pickering cites Vööbus enthusiastically;[8] but it is disappointing to observe that he fails to mention Matthew Black's decisive critique of Vööbus.[9] Black sees Rabbula as much less central in producing the Syriac Peshitta. Rabbula emerges as one of the links in the chain of its production, some of which are earlier than Rabbula, and others of which are later (the Peshitta did not thoroughly displace the Old Syriac until the sixth century). Thus even if Vööbus has rightly questioned the Rabbulan origins of the Peshitta version, it appears that Burkitt was entirely correct in seeing this version as a post-Nicene endeavor. And, intriguingly, the spread of textual affinities in the Peshitta — Byzantine, Western, Alexandrian — again testifies to the early fluidity of text-types; but it does not demonstrate that the Byzantine tradition in its mature conflated form existed in the ante-Nicene period. Meanwhile, we may well ask ourselves why, if the mature Byzantine text-

6. For a brief survey of such recent studies, cf. Bruce M. Metzger, *The Early Versions of the New Testament: Their Origin, Transmission and Limitations* (New York: Oxford University, 1977), pp. 60–63.

7. Cf. p. 46 (n. 4) above.

8. *The New Testament Text*, p. 90.

9. "Rabbula of Edessa and the Peshitta," *BJRL* 33 (1950–51): 203–10.

type were actually in common use in the ante-Nicene period, the other ancient versions (Old Latin, Old Syriac, Coptic, and so forth) either know nothing of it or make little use of it.

In short, there is still no hard evidence that the Byzantine text-type was known in the ante-Nicene period. But let me hasten to add that even if unambiguous evidence were found in support of its early existence, this would not prove its superiority. It would, to say the least, put it on the same footing as the other text-types; but it would not thereby *necessarily* be promoted to a position of supremacy.

Third, although Pickering rightly points out the importance of reconstructing a believable history of the text, he is persistently insensitive to the broader history in which the history of the text unfolds. He is right in asking that the rise of the Byzantine tradition be accounted for in a fashion that squares with the evidence. He is right when he points out that few accept the Hortian theory of a Lucianic recension at the base of the Byzantine text-type. He is right when he asks how various ante-Nicene Byzantine readings arose. But he is historically naive when he fails to discuss the significance of the professed conversion of Constantine, the immense influence of John Chrysostom in the eastern empire, the rise of monarchical bishops and their pressure for textual uniformity, the division of the Roman Empire and the demise of the Greek language (and the resulting preeminence of Latin) throughout the Mediterranean world, Byzantium excepted. Historically sensitive answers to questions like these may provide the true answer to the problem of why the text-type found in B or p^{75} was neglected for centuries.

When Pickering addresses himself directly to the question of how to account for the Byzantine text-type, however, he never raises such questions. His fundamental appeal, both in the body of his book and in its second appendix, is to probability statistics.[10] The basic argument is simple. If we grant that, on the average, each manuscript is copied the same number of times as the other manuscripts of its generation, then under normal circumstances the older the text-type the greater its

10. *The New Testament Text,* pp. 110-13, 149-59.

chances of surviving in a plurality or in a majority of the extant manuscripts of any later period. But since the oldest text-type is the autograph, it follows that this type must predominate.

This argument depends entirely on what Pickering calls "normal transmission." He repeatedly suggests that the rejection of his statistical argument entails a "radical" break from "normal transmission." But it is precisely at this point that Pickering is, in my view, historically naive. We may be sure that prototypes of the Byzantine text-type were circulating toward the middle of the fourth century; and it was this sort of text that Chrysostom[11] used in his immensely popular preaching in Antioch and Constantinople. It is entirely reasonable, historically speaking, to reconstruct the next one hundred years in terms of the effect of Chrysostom's popularity, the hardening of the Byzantine tradition, the restriction of the Greek language (by and large) to the incipient Byzantine Empire, and the massive displacement of Greek by Latin in the West. The simple convergence of a few such historical phenomena quite adequately accounts for the numerical superiority of the majority text. Granted this is so, then the statistical argument says nothing about the antiquity of the text at any point earlier than the fourth century. And if it says nothing about the text's ultimate antiquity, it equally says nothing about its authenticity.

Pickering introduces another wrinkle into the statistical argument. Suppose, he says, that a manuscript with an error were copied more times than another manuscript of the same generation without an error. It would follow that in the next generation there would be more "bad" copies than "good." But

---

11. On the text-type used by John Chrysostom, the best brief treatment is that of F. G. Kenyon, *The Text of the Greek Bible*, rev. A. W. Adams, 3d ed. (London: Duckworth, 1975), pp. 209ff. Adams rightly points out that Chrysostom's text "is by no means identical with the later and more or less established form of the ninth and tenth centuries. It may now be taken as an ascertained fact that there is a type of text which begins to make its appearance about the end of the fourth century, that this type in the course of time acquired predominance in the Church of Constantinople, and that it continued to be the text in general use throughout the Middle Ages, and finally was stereotyped in print" (p. 209). Adams's further discussion is most illuminating. See also Metzger, *The Early Versions*, p. 385.

suppose further that another error were introduced into one of the "bad" copies of this new generation. Even if this new, doubly-"bad" manuscript were copied more often than its peers, nevertheless in the next generation the new error would be found in a smaller number of manuscripts than those that retained the right reading, because all the thoroughly "good" manuscripts would join with the manuscripts that had only one "bad" reading to make up a majority witness against the second "bad" reading. In the long haul, therefore, as the number of generations increases, bad readings should be found in proportionately fewer manuscripts.

Again, however, I submit that this argument, whatever its reasonableness on paper, is historically naive. As Pickering himself points out, most errors were introduced into the manuscripts within the first two centuries.[12] Errors were not added one per generation, generation by generation, but wholesale, as it were. Pickering's statistical model therefore breaks down. If some of these corrupted manuscripts began to proliferate in an area where Greek was still the lingua franca, and therefore where many copies would be made because the demand would be greatest; and if there was concomitantly rising pressure to secure uniform copies of the New Testament (recall the injunction of Damasus to Jerome), then such basic historical considerations completely nullify Pickering's argument from probability statistics.

An analogy comes to mind, one that serves as a counterexample. One can erect a statistical model in which it is affirmed that there is, in any generation, a certain probability that each pair of parents will have, on average, so many children. This immediately suggests that the total number of offspring from parents of an early generation will outstrip the total number of offspring from parents of a later generation. Adam will have a greater number of descendants than Noah: indeed, he will have the greatest number of all. Similarly one might expect Lamech or Tubal-cain (Gen. 4) to have a greater number of descendants than Noah. According to Genesis, however, such reckoning is false: the "historical accident" of

12. *The New Testament Text*, p. 108.

the flood has eliminated that possibility. The mathematical model does not prove convincing once other historical factors are admitted. Similarly, Pickering's mathematical model does not prove convincing. And the use of mathematical symbols does not make his argument one iota stronger, as symbols could equally be used for my counterargument.

A concrete contradiction is in any case built into Pickering's argument about the tendencies of manuscript-copying in the first two centuries. On the one hand, as we have seen, Pickering admits what is generally agreed, that most variants existed before the end of the second century, including most of the worst corruptions. Of course he must concede this if he is to explain the uncials, minuscules, and papyri that he wishes to dismiss as corrupt. His resulting model of the history of the New Testament text[13] brings with it the unpleasant conclusion that the first two centuries of the Christian church can boast of the highest proportion of aberrant texts! Yet on the other hand Pickering elsewhere argues that the earliest believers would, on principle, extend the greatest care to their copying of manuscripts because they would reverence the New Testament writings the way the Jews reverenced their Hebrew Bible.[14]

Pickering has thus constructed a flat contradiction. The plain fact of the matter is that early Christians did not take nearly the pains with their Scriptures that the Jews did with theirs; and this is evidenced not only by the Christians' handling of the New Testament documents but also in their handling of the LXX. We may credit this to what we will—lack of education in some leaders, enthusiastic zeal that outran sober wisdom, the greatness of the demand, or whatever—but facts are facts. And the vast majority of the variants are not demonstrably the result of doctrinal prejudice so much as sheer carelessness.

In these and several other areas Pickering, it seems to me, is historically insensitive.

Fourth, Pickering has not dealt adequately with the papyri. He rightly points out that Byzantine readings are found in

---

13. Ibid., esp. p. 111.
14. Ibid., pp. 100–101.

p^{66}, whose textual affinities are, to say the least, highly erratic. Of course, as I indicated in my discussion of the fathers, early Byzantine readings do not necessarily argue for the presence of an early Byzantine text-type, and I need not repeat my argument. But although Pickering discusses erratic papyri like p^{66}, he does not anywhere discuss seriously the implications of the remarkable textual affinities of a papyrus like p^{75}. This papyrus agrees so closely with B, without apparently serving as its parent, that *text-type* is scarcely too strong a term to be used. Moreover, if the recent work by Gordon D. Fee is correct[15] (which Pickering does not discuss), then neither p^{75} nor B is recensional. If p^{75}, a second-century papyrus, is not recensional, then it must be either extremely close to the original or extremely corrupt. The latter possibility appears to be eliminated by the witness of B. If Fee's work stands up, then we must conclude that at least in John's Gospel the Alexandrian text-type is by far the closest to the autograph.

Fifth, Pickering cites the work of A. C. Clark[16] to the effect that in the transmission of classical Greek texts the error to which scribes were most prone was not interpolation but accidental omission. Applied to New Testament textual criticism, this could be taken to suggest that, all other things being equal, the longer reading should be assumed to be correct. Of course this would favor the Byzantine text-type. Most textual critics follow the opposite principle and, all things being equal, prefer the shorter reading *("brevior lectio potior")*.

In a footnote Pickering admits that Clark's work was criticized by F. G. Kenyon and others (he does not mention that the "others" were William Sanday and Alexander Souter), but he still believes Clark's work "has sufficient validity to be worth taking into account."[17] Unfortunately he does not detail the objections of Kenyon and the others; but the interested reader

15. Gordon D. Fee, "P^{75}, P^{66}, and Origen: The Myth of Early Textual Recension in Alexandria," in *New Dimensions in New Testament Study,* ed. Richard N. Longenecker and Merrill C. Tenney (Grand Rapids: Zondervan, 1974), pp. 19–45.

16. A. C. Clark, *The Descent of Manuscripts* (Oxford: Clarendon, 1918); cf. Pickering, *The New Testament Text,* p. 80.

17. *The New Testament Text,* p. 172 (n. 148).

may turn with profit to the brief treatments in the standard works.[18] More unfortunate yet, Pickering does not mention that Clark himself applied his theory to the famous textual problem of Acts, supporting as a result the longer Western form of the text over against the Byzantine! However, after undergoing rigorous criticism by some of his colleagues, Clark returned some years later to the question of the textual traditions underlying Acts, and to all intents and purposes abandoned his former theory in favor of another, namely, that Luke himself had produced two editions of Acts. On this theory too he faced serious challenge; but the chronicling of this later dispute would transport us beyond the concerns of textual criticism per se. Clark's work on scribal habits, however, does not appear to be so crucial after all.

More work needs to be done in this area of scribal tendencies; but the generalization offered by Pickering and Clark (and B. H. Streeter before them) certainly needs, to say the least, serious qualification. For a start, a distinction would have to be made between accidental and nonaccidental changes. And there are other questions to answer. For example, in the area of intentional changes, would early, reverent Christians be quicker to risk losing sacred words than to risk preserving words that were not sacred but not obviously harmful or untrue? Certainly the later institutional church preferred the latter risk!

Sixth, The criticism I just offered pinpoints a much broader weakness in Pickering's work. Although he is much more fair and restrained than many defenders of the Byzantine tradition, nevertheless in my view he still spends too much time erecting and knocking down straw men, overstating his case, and even unfairly quoting from his opponents. I offer a representative list of examples:

1. Pickering cites authors who insist that the recovery of the original text of the Bible is impossible.[19] "At this point," he

---

18. E.g., Metzger, *The Text of the New Testament: Its Transmission, Corruption, and Restoration,* 2d ed. (New York: Oxford University, 1968), pp. 161-63; Kenyon, *The Text of the Greek Bible,* pp. 237-38.

19. *The New Testament Text,* pp. 18-19.

says, "I get uncomfortable. If the original wording is lost and gone forever, whatever are we using? The consequences of such an admission are so far-reaching, to my mind, that a thorough review of the evidence is called for." But this approach projects a distorted image in the mind of the reader, an image that suggests that accepting the Byzantine text entails faithfulness to the Word of God and recovery of the original words of Scripture, and rejecting the Byzantine text cuts a person free from all possibility of knowing God's will. I have already dealt with this under theses 9 and 12. Suffice it to add this additional remark: Pickering himself later admits that following his approach still stops short of ultimate proof that we have the original wording,[20] Only the autographs could provide such confidence. As I indicated earlier, even within the Byzantine tradition no two manuscripts agree perfectly There is a difference only of degree between the variations found within a textual tradition and the variations scattered across two or more text-types. In that sense it is entirely correct that, as some authors cited by Pickering have argued,[21] we can never achieve perfect certainty on the precise wording of the entire New Testament; and that point stands firm regardless of whether the Byzantine text be followed or not. Of course most of the New Testament is already textually certain; and as I have already argued, the remaining variations may affect the interpretation of various passages, but they do not affect a single doctrine.

2. Pickering's criticisms of eclecticism are sometimes unfair.[22] Even the criticisms offered by Eldon Jay Epp and others are generally actually directed at its worst practitioners; and if I understand Epp correctly, although he rightly pinpoints the many weaknesses of eclecticism (real or potential), he nevertheless offers no better method. His comments are presented as a goad to make us aware of weaknesses and to spur us on to more research in order to achieve greater precision. It is true that eclecticism, to be final, would require omniscient textual

20. Ibid., p. 144.
21. Ibid., pp. 18–19.
22. Ibid., pp. 24ff.

critics;[23] but it does not follow that the pursuit of truth should be abandoned in favor of opting for one part of the evidence. In principle the same omniscience would be required to make sound judgments about variants even within the Byzantine textual tradition. Pickering's entire treatment of eclecticism would have more credibility if, with Epp and others, he could see its weaknesses without parodying it.

3. Again and again, Pickering mentions the fact that most manuscripts within the Byzantine tradition have not been neatly related genealogically to others within the same tradition. But he jumps from this fact to the proposition that they are therefore "independent witnesses."[24] That simply does not follow! Precise connections may well have been lost; more links may yet be discovered. In principle, because every manuscript but the original is a copy of at least one other, and perhaps of several others, genealogical relationships must exist. As I have already indicated, the questions to be asked are: If a manuscript were copied from several others, *could* the precise relationships be detected, granted the abundance of attendant witnesses? But all these individual manuscripts cannot be justly said to be independent. Some of them *may* be; but the point must not be assumed.

4. There are too many glib statements, statements not quite true. For example, Pickering tells us it is "common knowledge that all the earliest MSS, the ones upon which our critical texts are based, come from Egypt."[25] In fact we do not know where B and D came from; and certain manuscripts of ancient versions do not boast Egyptian provenance. Again, Pickering speaks of "the known existence of a variety of maliciously altered texts in the second century;"[26] but his ensuing discussion refers to accidental and careless errors such as itacistic spellings.

23. Ibid., pp. 24, 125
24. Ibid., p. 54; cf. pp. 52, 89, 131–32, 134.
25. Ibid., p. 116
26. Ibid.

5. Pickering argues that manuscripts from one geographical area cannot be considered independent witnesses and therefore must be given, collectively, precisely one vote.[27] I am astonished that a person who can see weaknesses in Hort's genealogical principle cannot see similar weaknesses compounded in his own geographical principle. Pickering is attempting to use this argument to reduce all the witnesses from Egypt to one vote — despite the vast diversity in the textual traditions preserved in Egypt. Incidentally the reason Egypt has brought forth so many ancient manuscripts is that her climate is hot and dry, ideal for preserving such things. But the richness of her textual heritage, far from indicating a provincial isolationism, is strong evidence that she reflected textual traditions from all parts of the empire. Moreover all these finds from Egypt are very early; so when Pickering points out that the relatively uniform Byzantine cursives spring from many countries stretching from Greece to England and from Africa to Gaul, he should in all fairness also point out the following: (1) Not one of them is as early as the non-Byzantine uncials and papyri. (2) Most of them are at least five hundred years later, and some of them one thousand years later. (3) Although they are found in many countries now, in fact we do not know of their ultimate origin; but not a few spread from Constantinople throughout the Mediterranean world during the Renaissance, which followed hard on the heels of the collapse of the Byzantine Empire. And (4) most of those whose origins are truly found in non-Byzantine cities are late copies of manuscripts preserved in the Byzantine Empire; and they were copied at a time when scribes had little choice, ignorant as they were of the later finds of uncials and papyri.

Seventh, I am uncertain what relevance the appendix on 7Q5 has for the thrust of Pickering's book as a whole. In this appendix Pickering argues in favor of O'Callaghan's identification of 7Q5 with Mark 6:52-53, and against O'Callaghan's critics (especially Maurice Baillet).[28] But as I say, I remain

27. Ibid., p. 133.

28. Maurice Baillet, "Les manuscrits de la grotte 7 de Qumrân et le Nouveau Testament," *Bib* 53 (1972): 508-16; 54 (1973): 340-50.

uncertain as to the relevance of this appendix to the book as a whole.

In any case, in establishing one's own position it is seldom helpful to focus all attention on the most extreme opposition. Perhaps Baillet's criticisms of O'Callaghan are overdone; yet there are plenty of very sober-minded critics around who remain doubtful that O'Callaghan has proved his point. For example, C. J. Hemer does not insist that O'Callaghan's reconstruction is impossible; but he does show that it is at best speculative and that it could fit other passages just as well.[29] I do not believe that conservative biblical scholarship is helped along its way when every potential conservative find is hailed swiftly or uncritically.

In drawing this appendix to a close, Pickering writes: "It seems to me that 7Q5, 4 and 8 tend to confirm the history of the text presented in this volume. That someone should have a collection of New Testament writings at such an early date confirms their early recognition as Scripture and implies an early notion of a N.T. canon."[30]

I remain unpersuaded that 7Q5 is any sort of basis on which to build propositions concerning the early recognition of New Testament documents as Scripture—propositions that in my view, find much better support elsewhere. However, even if 7Q5 did attest a high view of New Testament documents and an early notion of New Testament canon, it baffles me to see how such attestation in any sense would confirm Pickering's history of the New Testament text. O'Callaghan is not suggesting that 7Q5 contains a Byzantine reading!

That brings me to my final criticism:

Eighth, as do many other defenders of the Byzantine text-type, Pickering ultimately tries to forge a necessary connection between his understanding of textual criticism and a high view of Scripture. Pickering is more careful than most in this regard; but the concluding remarks to his second appendix (on 7Q5) and his entire first appendix ("Inspiration and Preserva-

---

29. "New Testament Fragments at Qumran?" *TB* 23 (1972): 125-28; "A Note on 7Q5," *ZNW* 65 (1974): 155-57.

30. *The New Testament Text,* p. 148.

tion"), give away this perspective in the end. But as in other writers, so in Pickering: the connection is based on assertion without evidence, on affirmation without serious theological reflection. I have already dealt with this question under theses 5, 9, and 12, and beg the reader's indulgence if I do not repeat those arguments here. I need only add that *even if* the Byzantine text-type were one day demonstrated to be closer to the autographs than the other textual traditions (an eventuality of which, at this point, I can scarcely conceive), belief in traditional formulations of biblical inspiration would not be affected in the slightest. This granted, the defenders of the Byzantine tradition ought to desist from all statements suggesting or implying that defenders of any other view necessarily risk a heterodox view of Scripture.

Index

Of Authors

Index of Authors

Of Scripture